D1433397

HAWKER

The story of the 125

Bill Gunston

HAWKER

The story of the 125

Bill Gunston

Edited by Mike Brown
Picture consultant: Phil Birtles

Airworthy Publications
International Limited

First published in 1996 in Great Britain by
Airworthy Publications International Limited,
Bassfield South, Manchester Road,
Walmersley, Bury, Lancashire BL9 5LY.

Copyright © Airworthy Publications
International Limited

ISBN 0 952 8845 0X

Publisher's acknowledgement

The publishers would like to express their grateful thanks to British Aerospace and Raytheon Corporate Jets for their support in enabling this definitive history of the 125 to be published. We would especially like to thank Mike Brown, Philip Birtles and David McIntosh for invaluable help and advice during the design of the book.

The photographs have largely been furnished by Raytheon Corporate Jets, the majority coming from the archives previously owned by British Aerospace. Those on pages 3, 10, 13, 20, 23, 24, 26, 30, 43, 49, 50, 56, 57, 58, 64, 76 and 94 were taken by Philip Birtles, and others are from his private collection. Photograph on page 2 courtesy of Aer Lingus; page 44 Marshall Aerospace and the three on page 45 Racal Radar Defence Systems.

Three-view General Arrangements in the Appendices redrawn by Richard Gardner; artist's impression on page 3 redrawn by Sable Illustration.

Other research by Steve Broadbent.

Book designed by Viv Harper.

Reproduction by EPC Direct, Bristol.

Printed and bound in Italy.

A Hawker 1000 makes a dramatic departure from an airfield in the United States.

Author's preface

Bill Gunston

Some thirty years ago the de Havilland Aircraft Company thought they could sell their new executive jet for £100,000, ($150,000 at today's rates). Today a Hawker 1000 will set you back a cool $13,000,000. Although this is many times more than the difference due to inflation today's customers for this famous aeroplane are getting a lot more 'plane for their money, and are being taken for a ride only in the nicest, most literal sense.

The original guesstimated selling price was, as is often the case in aerospace, almost certainly a gross underestimate. At exactly the same time another famous British company, Avro, launched the 748 twin-turboprop and really did lose a great deal of money by under-pricing it. But by far the most important reason for the rise in the price of the Hawker is that today's version does five times the job of the first aircraft.

It flies faster, though that is seldom of great importance. It has far more room, and a much better interior. From the operator's viewpoint, the most significant change is that the range has been multiplied by three! Noise has been slashed by roughly 95 per cent. Not least, its appearance has been transformed. One early non-customer rejected the Hawker in 1965 because, he said, it looked "like the back of a Mack truck". Today a Ferrari might be more appropriate.

I was delighted to have been asked to write this book. The Hawker is not merely a success story but a success story that I think will set records.

The DC-3 has become a legend, but all of them were pretty much alike and they were only in production for nine years. There are many other famous passenger/transport aircraft, but – apart from the Soviet An-2 biplane, flown in 1947 and until recently still in production in China – I cannot think of any that can rival the ongoing success story of the Hawker.

Today's Hawker 800 and Hawker 1000 are the products of 35 years of effort. The following story thus distils the work of countless designers, engineers, commercial specialists and top management. Some are still in harness, others have retired to their country retreats, while many, sadly, are no longer able to tell me about their work. I hope that few of the major characters in this story have been omitted. If any have, it was not for the want of much research. This applies especially to the incomplete recorded history of the first ten years. The omissions of history result from the single-minded concentration on the job, which was getting the aircraft flying and into service. Some companies actually have historians or archivists; I urge them not to overlook the need to record everything as it happens.

Bill Gunston
Haslemere, Surrey, England, 1996.

Editor's Preface

Mike Brown

When Bill Gunston first wrote the text for this book, incredibly in the space of just a couple of weeks or so, the Hawker 1000 was a newly launched programme "still on the drawing board" and the 125 was an integral, and profitable, part of British Aerospace's Commercial Aircraft business, along with the BAe 146, ATP, Jetstream and wings for the European Airbus.

The fact that it was written in such a short space of time is testimony to Bill's legendary writing speed, not to any lack of research into the detail, which preceded. This I can attest to as he spent many a day sitting in my office at Hatfield, papers and files spread over a large table, as he delved into the background to the story.

At the time publication was delayed in the desire to check the accuracy of the facts as much as possible – a time-consuming business as it entailed contacting many ex-employees who had been intimately involved in the programme but who had since retired to remote parts of the country. With the major changes to the business that then developed it was decided to hold publication until things had settled down. But the problem with an ongoing story is that it never ends and the last chapter is out of date almost as soon as the final full point is inserted. Since we had to put our peg in the ground at some time, Bill was asked to come back to Hatfield in 1995 to rewrite the last three chapters. Additionally, I had to do some editing to some of the existing text to reflect the programme's new ownership, do some final updating just prior to going to print, and also research the appendices. I hope that my alterations do no more than make for a smooth read and do not despoil Bill's prose.

I must also record my thanks to Phil Birtles for his considerable efforts in double-checking the text for factual errors and supplying and captioning a number of the photographs that appear in this book. Phil is an acknowledged expert in "things de Havilland" and is an author in his own right. He worked for many years at Hatfield, both as PA to the legendary John Cunningham and in the Public Relations department, so he can claim some close association with this subject.

Because the name of the aircraft has changed a number of times over the years, reflecting the various changes in parent company, it was decided in the interests of historical accuracy to use the name current at the period being recorded in each chapter.

Mike Brown
Raytheon Aircraft Company
Hatfield & Harrow, 1996

Contents

How it all started...

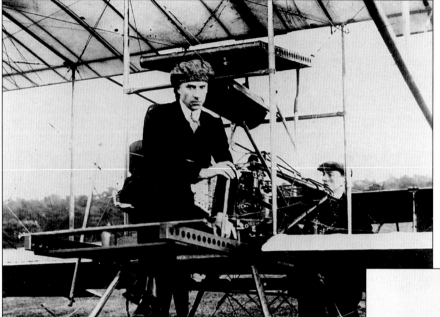

Geoffrey de Havilland designed and built his first aircraft in 1909, powered by an engine of his own design. However, with his inexperience in flying, it resulted in a crash on its first attempt at flight in December, only the engine being salvaged. His second design was more successful, making its first hop of about 18 metres on 10 September 1910. This aircraft became the first purchased by the British Government in December when de Havilland and his colleague Frank Hearle joined the Royal Aircraft Factory (RAF) at Farnborough.

His duties here were as an aircraft designer and test pilot, and Geoffrey's most successful design was the B.E. series starting with the B.E.1, a "reconstruction" from a Voisin biplane, the only connection being the engine. Geoffrey made the first flight on 27 December 1911, gaining the height record of 3,218m on 12 August 1912 carrying a passenger. The aircraft was later developed into the highly successful B.E.2 series, produced during the early part of World War 1. His last design for Farnborough was B.S.1.

With the design and manufacture of aircraft allocated to the private companies, Geoffrey de Havilland left Farnborough and joined the Aircraft Manufacturing Company (Airco) at Hendon on 2 July 1914 as Chief Designer and Test Pilot. Here he started the D.H. series with D.H.1, a two-seat reconnaissance aircraft, which first flew in January 1915. It had a 120hp Beardmore pusher engine, the observer sat in the front cockpit, and a total of 73 were built.

Airco later closed, but the de Havilland Aircraft Company was started at the Stag Lane Aerodrome, Edgware (north London) on 25 September, 1920. The design and manufacturing activities followed the de Havilland Flying School to Hatfield in 1934.

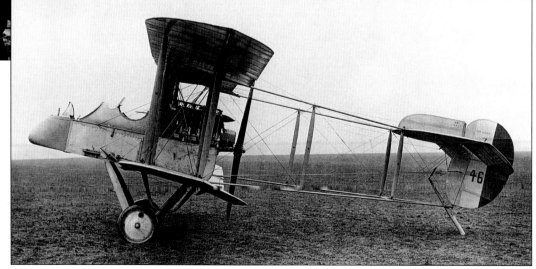

1
Getting it right

One day in 1961 Martin Sharp, the Public Relations Manager of the de Havilland Aircraft Company, was sitting in his office at Hatfield writing copy for the first press release announcing the existence of the D.H.125. Like all long-serving D.H. people, Martin had a great sense of history. He wrote, "The new jet, which is the 125th★ de Havilland design, is named the Dragon in honour of the historic and unforgettable D.H.84 of 1932. The D.H.125 will be called the Jet Dragon until the time, not far ahead, when the adjective will be thought to have become needless". Later he stuck his neck out and wrote, "The Dragon project follows a worldwide study of market needs. It is a purely commercial venture, involving an investment of several million pounds, justified by the belief that it may well remain in production and in use for as long as 20 years".

★ *(Not strictly true as de Havilland omitted the D.H.13 from its design numbering sequence. The 125 was thus technically the 124th D.H. design. – Ed.)*

He would have loved to have lived to read this book. Today the Hawker, as the 125 is now called, has been in production well over 30 years and there is every reason to believe it will still be in production in its 40th year. Given that many of the early series aircraft are still in regular operation after 30 years of service, it is likely that Hawkers will still be flying at least 70 years after the first flight in 1962. Not many

The D.H.125 was originally to have been called the "Jet Dragon" – this is the original type to be named "Dragon", the D.H.84, an elegant passenger-carrying biplane of the 1930s.

This superb example, owned by Aer Lingus, has recently undergone a six-year restoration in Dublin. The photo (left) is courtesy Aer Lingus, and the aircraft was photographed (right) by Philip Birtles at Woburn, England, on 18 August 1996. Orignally EI-AFK, it has been restored as EI-ABI to represent the first aircraft operated by Aer Lingus.

aircraft, anywhere in the world, at any time in history, can make such a claim. Indeed, in terms of jet aircraft, the Hawker probably holds the record.

The key to it, of course, is product improvement, but you have to have a sound basic product with which to start. Since the first Hawker there have been several executive jets which have fallen by the wayside, and several more which have experienced prolonged difficulties. In contrast, if you ask any old-timer on the Hawker programme about faults and problems he may be hard put to think of anything really serious. The Hawker just started well and got progressively better.

That is not to claim that the first Hawker was perfect. The de Havilland company had a reputation for making things simple. If a signal could be sent by joining things with a piece of string, then that was better than complex electronics (not to be taken too literally!). The first Hawker was a very basic aircraft, and a little of this showed in its appearance. But it was good enough to sell and get the production line going, and

from then onwards the only place for the Hawker to go was up. In the things that really mattered, the features that would have been very difficult and costly to alter, the Hawker was almost spot-on.

On the other hand, the birth of the Hawker was very far from being all sweetness and light. The de Havilland company had a long heritage of selling business and executive aircraft, including many to the British monarchy and to other heads of state. The first true business aircraft from de Havilland was probably the D.H.80A Puss Moth of 1930. Certainly one of the most successful was the post-war D.H.104 Dove, a trim six-seater first flown in 1945. This eventually sold to a total of 542, but towards the late 1950s orders were beginning to come in very slowly.

Part of the trouble was that the D.H. Gipsy Queen engines were becoming dated, and there were many people at Hatfield who advocated merely replacing them with Lycomings or Continentals. The more fundamental problem was that the world's airlines were swiftly re-equipping with jets, and a piston-engined executive aircraft was becoming an anachronism. Before the end of the 1950s it was crystal clear that de Havilland either had to follow the Dove with a turboprop or jet aircraft,

or else give up the executive and light-transport sector entirely.

By then de Havilland had become a dedicated manufacturer of jet airliners. It had, after all, set the ball rolling with the world's first jet airliner, the Comet, which made its maiden flight from Hatfield in May, 1949. The first move towards a smaller jet had been in the winter of 1956-57, when Chief Designer C.T. (Tim) Wilkins had roughed out a general-arrangement drawing of what at that time was a new idea, an executive jet. Use of gas-turbine engines, no matter whether turbojets or turboprops, automatically called for the aircraft to cruise at high altitude in order to achieve reasonable fuel economy, and this in turn meant a pressurised cabin. Thus Wilkins drew a cigar-shaped fuselage, carrying two Bristol Orpheus turbojets, each of about 4,800 lb thrust, at the rear.

Nothing more happened to this particular concept, but it was later joined by others. The company was deeply imbued with a wish not only to keep things simple but also to keep them cheap. The lowest-cost approach to the notion of an executive jet was clearly to use the de Havilland Vampire, or rather Vampire Trainer, as a basis. It was soon found that the existing side-by-side nacelle of this mass-produced aircraft could be replaced by a larger structure seating, typically, a pilot and up to four passengers. Officially called the Communicator, it was more often referred to as the Executor or Excavator. This too remained a paper project, but it is worth noting that as recently as 1987 a company called JetCraft USA was trying to do precisely the same thing to a Vampire in Las Vegas.

All the time intelligence was flowing into Hatfield from the de Havilland sales representatives all over the world. By far the most important input, because it came from by far the biggest market, was that from Ian Fossett. He was a former Hatfield pilot who had been appointed President of de Havilland Aircraft Inc, the US company formed to sell and support the Dove. Almost all customers considered the Dove's accommodation, for side-by-side pilots separated by a light bulkhead from a six-seat cabin, to be just about right. Equally universal was the requirement for more speed and range. Either of these demands meant a more powerful aircraft, and almost certainly a heavier one, and combined with greater speeds and manoeuvring loads this implied a

much stronger structure. This again meant greater weight, and, whereas the Dove Mk.8 weighed 8,950 lb loaded, the Future Projects staff at Hatfield, led by Derek Brown, found it hard to keep a turbine-powered replacement under 12,500 lb, the statutory limit for single-pilot operation. In any case there were many other projects being studied at Hatfield – for everything from supersonic VTOL (vertical takeoff and landing) fighters to DC-3 replacements – that were better defined and had higher priority.

In March 1958 Fossett, sensing the hardening of attitudes at the top against developments of the Dove, collaborated closely with Future Projects on possible new turboprop and jet aircraft to meet the growing needs of customers around the world. One proposal, later handled by the team at de Havilland's Christchurch factory (on the south coast of England near Bournemouth) under W.A. "Bill" Tamblin, was a study for an aircraft powered by two Gnome turboprops. This engine was a 1,150 shp turboprop derivation of the de Havilland-licensed version of the General Electric T58 turboshaft engine. The aircraft would have had a fuselage diameter of 81 inches, cruising speed of 400 mph and range of 1,750 miles, and it was hoped to stay within "the 12,500 lb barrier". But the emergence of the military JetStar and Sabreliner in the USA soon made Fossett convinced that, in the 1960s, no propeller aircraft could compete. In May 1958 drawings were done of an aircraft powered by two General Electric J85 turbojets, each of 2,850 lb thrust, followed in July by a similar aircraft powered by Armstrong Siddeley (later Bristol Siddeley) Vipers. The Vipers developed for civil use were much heavier, and only gave around 2,500 lb thrust.

In 1959 Fossett talked again with many North American and other Dove operators, and in the summer of that year he laid down the firm guidelines for a full company project to be known as the D.H.125. It had to fly at 500 mph, cross the United States with one stop, and have stand-up headroom and a toilet. The speed obviously meant jet engines

Right: de Havilland effectively pioneered the concept of business aircraft starting with the D.H.80A Puss Moth of the early thirties. The highly successful D.H.104 Dove (depicted, left) set the standard for post-war business aviation. Production of the Dove was phased out in favour of the D.H.125.

and, as is explained at the start of Chapter 8, there were clear advantages in fuel economy and lack of noise in using turbofans instead of "straight" turbojets. But in 1959 noise and fuel burn were nothing like as important as they are today, and though the project staff carried on a flirtation with the 4,200 lb thrust General Electric CF700 until 1963, the only engines really seriously considered were turbojets, as described later.

The late 1950s were a time of rapid change, and much argument. One potential customer for a new aircraft was the Royal Air Force, which from 1958 discussed with de Havilland the best way of replacing its Avro Anson, D.H. Dove and Vickers Varsity aircraft, all used for either liaison or navigation training (in the case of the Anson, both). At that time the RAF favoured a turboprop, but interest in a jet was kindled by Philip Lucas, the former Hawker Aircraft Company test pilot who became D.H. Technical Sales Manager. More heated arguments on the

An artist's impression of the D.H.125, published in about 1960, before the design was finalised.

An early concept illustration of the D.H.125 "Jet Dragon" showing the original tailplane arrangement without any overfin.

likely to result in greater first cost, more interior noise and vibration, and less potential for development. Occasionally a customer was encountered who professed to be unconcerned about speed. One such was Shell, visited in early 1960. But on 12 March 1960 a meeting was held with "Splinter" Spirenberg, manager of the big fleet of executive aircraft operated by the giant Dutch company Philips of Eindhoven. He was totally uncompromising and virtually wrote the specification for the 125, stipulating jet speed, and ability to fly at high altitude over the weather with a high standard of interior comfort.

A confidential report compiled by de Havilland at this time showed that the anticipated market was for 200 aircraft, a modest number for the company which had been used to production runs of many hundreds, if not thousands. The report, which looked at various options for de Havillands to pursue, supported a twin-jet solution for an executive

An early interior concept for six seats.

merits of turboprops versus jets were carried on in *Flight* magazine (your author was Technical Editor at the time), by Frank Robertson (Shorts) and Bob Whitby (BEA), who both championed propellers, and de Havilland's Richard M. Clarkson (Research Director) and David R. Newman (Chief Aerodynamicist), who supported jets. In the case of corporate aircraft, history suggests that the jet protagonists got it right.

Nevertheless, at the time the question was wide open. Clarkson battled for the jet 125 as he battled for the jet D.H.126 feederliner (DC-3 replacement) against the twin-Gnome D.H.123. During the three crucial years 1958-60 it was Fossett who said what form the 125 should take, and Clarkson who persistently kept the project alive against powerful opposing forces, which at one time even managed temporarily to forbid him to do any further work on the projected 125. (In 1969 his work was recognised by the award of the Mullard Medal by the Royal Society.)

Admittedly, turboprops burned less fuel, but studies showed that, apart from not meeting the crucial US demand for speed, they were aircraft. The report stated, however, "It is true that either of these aeroplanes (the Gnome Executive and the Jet Executive) fall into a category as yet unfilled by the American market, insofar as the competing US aircraft are all either far more expensive or much slower. It does not, however, follow that such a market exists, and we personally would feel very doubtful about committing D.H. Hatfield to the design *de novo* of an aeroplane aimed at the highly competitive American executive market, and having very limited prospects on this side of the Atlantic, in the face of competition from perfectly adequate aeroplanes such as the Astazou-powered Dove and its European competitors at less than half the price."

The 125 was having a shaky hand-to-mouth existence, with nobody actually assigned to it, and with virtually no support from Marketing, apart from Fossett. Its credibility was further damaged by the fact that it had been repeatedly put up to the company board by Clarkson and

been repeatedly rejected. It might never have got started at all had not the British Government decided in April 1960 to abandon the British Blue Streak long-range ballistic missile and replace it with the American Skybolt (which was subsequently abandoned by the United States).

Loss of Blue Streak meant no work for large numbers of de Havilland engineers. It was Sir Geoffrey de Havilland himself who said, "We must quickly find work for these men, I suggest we get on with the executive jet". Accordingly the design responsibility for the 125 was transferred to the project staff in the Design Department. Here everyone was a designer with great ideas in mind. Within hours, Wilkins had assembled a team of six experienced structural designers under C.J. (Joe) Goodwin, who moved from being Structural Designer, Blue Streak, to become Designer-in-Charge, D.H.125.

In January 1960, reacting to pressure from the government, the entire

The fuselage for aircraft 25001 is off-loaded from a transporter in the Hatfield Erecting Shop following its journey from Chester. Note the first of the D.H.121 Tridents on the line in the background.

First of 500?

1962 was a golden year of the British aircraft industry. Two civil airliners had made their first flights earlier in the year – the D.H.121 Trident from Hatfield on 9 January, and the Vickers VC.10 from Weybridge on 29 June: among many other milestones, the Avro 748 entered service, the first flight of the BAC One-Eleven was imminent and development work was underway on the Anglo-French Concorde.

Military and light aircraft, engine and missile projects also flourished, and research aircraft such as the Bristol 188 (first flight 14 April 1962), Hunting H.126 and Handley Page H.P.115 seemed to abound.

Great things were expected of the industry, and the staff of *Flight International* – the "International" was added at the start of the year – had no shortage of "home" news with which to fill their pages, Significantly, the year also saw the first flight of the Boeing 727 and the first announcements of what became the McDonnell Douglas DC.9.

It would not have been surprising, therefore, if the first flight of the D.H.125 had been largely ignored, but *Flight International* sent along its reporter, and devoted a two-page spread to the event, under the headline "First of 500?"

Noting that G-ARYA had made a taxi run and "had hopped" the previous day, the report mentions the high speed taxi run on the morning of Monday, 13 August, and then "a sumptuous

luncheon is served. D.H. Top People sit at the top table.... She takes off at 2.50pm in less than 2000 feet and climbs confidently away on a dead straight course to the north-east.... Fifty minutes later she returns for a fly-past. She looks elegant."

"As she touches down, a senior D.H. salesman is heard to remark, "well, there she is, the first of 500?" He could well be right, if the 125 sells as well as the D.H.104 Dove, still in production after 17 years and a run of 529." (The Dove went on to 542.)

Most aircraft salesmen are optimists. As it turned out, the one quoted was unusually pessimistic, for the 125 passed 500 deliveries after less than 20 years, and by the time the last aircraft rolls off the line at Chester, early in 1997, almost 950 will have been assembled there. And, of course, production continues in the USA.

The first D.H.125, G-ARYA, pictured on a test flight on 8 November 1962. Note the flight test sensors on the forward fuselage.

de Havilland enterprise had become part of the giant Hawker Siddeley engineering group. It was this move which subsequently was to trigger the name now used for the 125. Much later, in 1965, the member companies of this group – such famous names as Armstrong Whitworth, Gloster, Folland, Blackburn and Avro, as well as D.H. – were to lose their identities entirely. For the moment the take-over had no tangible effect at Hatfield, which became the de Havilland Division under Air Commodore F.R. (Rod) Banks.

The D.H.125 design group naturally started where Clarkson left off. At the end of April 1960 the latest 125 drawing had shown an aft-engined, T-tailed design with wing spars passing straight through the 84-inch diameter fuselage. This resulted in a flat-floor twin jet with a slightly swept wing and a fuselage which was wide enough for three seats abreast. Wilkins liked the fat fuselage; Fossett repeatedly stressed the need for stand-up headroom, and Wilkins measured well over 6 feet. But he was also, as a lifetime D.H. man, deeply conscious of the wish to save money – not in a miserly way but to offer the aircraft at a lower price. He was already concerned that the Dove, originally priced at under £20,000, was in 1960 selling for twice that sum. The notion of a Turbine Dove was still an active project – and was to remain so until after 1966 – and Wilkins was determined that the price of the D.H.125 should be not more than a little over twice the latest Dove price.

Accordingly, Wilkins' first instruction to his 125 project design group was, "Get it under 12,500 lb". It was appreciated that the high cruising speed of a jet meant shorter times, and as nobody was thinking in terms of trips longer than a few hundred miles there seemed little real need for passengers to move about. Thus, there was no need for refreshment facilities or a toilet. Having designed the D.H.106 Comet and D.H.121 Trident, the latter having been first designed big and then foolishly made smaller on the instructions of the customer, Wilkins knew that, at least where commercial transports are concerned, a big aircraft costs little more than a small one and represents better value for money. But for an executive jet, not strictly an earner of revenue, it was thought different

G-ARYA is rolled out at Hatfield for its first exposure to the press.

Chris Capper (left) and fellow test pilot Geoffrey Pike, who shared much of the early development flying on the D.H.125.

rules applied. Though Fossett, by this time the worldwide Sales Manager, Executive Aircraft, continued to insist on a walk-around interior plus toilet and galley, there remained a colossal urge to keep the 125 simple and cheap.

The little design group never got near 12,500 lb, even with a fuselage so constricted that a bulged dome was added to enable passengers to stand upright at the toilet! Most of the designers heaved a sigh of relief when the 125 was permitted to grow back to 15,000 lb, and then to 16,500 lb. This enabled the fuselage diameter to recover near to the original, at 76 inches; the overall dimensions came back almost exactly

to where they had been in Future Projects in early May. But in one respect there had been a big change.

Mainly to save money in the water-tank pressure-test programme, it was decided not to run the spars through the fuselage but to sit the complete cylindrical fuselage on top of the wing. It was soon confirmed that the centre section could be slightly dished without losing spar strength, and that the wing could be built in one piece and faired in satisfactorily. As a bonus, there was no obstructive step in the cabin, the circular section giving the required stand-up headroom along the aisle of the cabin. This resulted in an unusual appearance, and also

The prototype G-ARYA returns from its maiden flight at Hatfield where the first two aircraft were assembled. The enthusiastic crowd welcomes back Chris Capper, the test pilot in charge of the original development programme.

necessitated an under-fuselage skid for safety in a wheels-up landing.

Some people were concerned about the aerodynamic drag of the arrangement. One in particular was Hawker Siddeley's Technical Director S.D. "Cock" Davies, and he repeatedly asked Wilkins and Newman for reassurance. In fact, Davies was right; tunnel testing had been done at low Reynolds Numbers, and the extra drag aft of the ultra-low wing did not show up until the actual aircraft was flying. Gradually successive versions of 125 got the shape right.

In any case, no attempt was made to emulate the Mach 0.88 cruising speed of the D.H.121 Trident. After consideration of many variables, including the later emergence of faster competitors, the design cruising Mach Number was fixed at 0.725. This equates with an EAS of 290 knots, which means a TAS of 500 mph (435 knots) at around 25,000 feet. This was judged near the upper limit for the kind of basic aeroplane de Havilland was anxious to create. It enabled the wing to be designed with an almost straight trailing edge and only 25 degrees of sweep on the leading edge, and yet have the deep thickness/chord ratio of 14 per cent at the root. In turn this meant a light and inexpensive structure with ample internal volume for fuel. With double-slotted flaps it was possible to reduce approach speeds to 86 knots, enabling the 125 to operate with room to spare from rough airstrips 4,500 feet long.

A further important result of the modest cruising speed was that it enabled flight controls to be manual throughout. This saved a great deal of weight and cost, but in fact probably added considerably to the bill for flight testing. The tailplane (horizontal stabiliser) was not pivoted, but was fixed to the top of the fin. As had often been the case with Hatfield aircraft, the fin was too small. This had been warned against and later confirmed by tunnel testing, and as there was an aerodynamically sluggish region under the rear fuselage, especially at high angles of attack, the required extra area was added as an overfin on top of the horizontal surface. It was designed in time to fly on the first aircraft. Most people think this improved the appearance. Another advantage was the auto rudder-bias system described in the next chapter.

As had been done in Future Projects, Wilkins' team looked at alternative configurations, but eventually came back to the one they started with. A low wing, which automatically meant rear-mounted

G-ARYA about to touch down at Hatfield after an early test flight.

engines, minimised structure weight and cost. It also improved appearance, was preferable in a wheels-up landing, seemed likely almost to eliminate engine FOD (foreign-object damage), and made possible traditional over-wing gravity refuelling. The chosen body diameter resulted in a cabin 72 inches wide and 69 inches high at the centreline, compared with the corresponding Dove dimensions of 54 and 62 inches. The seats were mounted on raised ledges on each side, the aisle being 8 inches lower. The first brochure described how this made it easier for passengers to sit down, stand up or talk to people standing in the aisle. Cabin length from the bulkhead behind the flight deck to the rear pressure bulkhead was fixed at 19 feet 8 inches, about 2 feet longer than in the Dove.

The main entrance door was naturally placed ahead of the wing, just behind the flight deck. As the sill height was only 40 inches, there was no problem in arranging for lightweight folding airstairs to be provided,

though this was totally unconnected with the door, which was designed to pull in and slide upwards, rotating around the circular frames. Opposite the door, on the right side, there was avionics racking at floor level, with stowage for baggage above. Ahead of the door, backing on to the flight-deck bulkhead, a small galley was provided.

Hydraulic, electric and fuel systems were all designed to be as simple as possible. For airframe de-icing the final choice was the TKS system, in which an alcohol-based fluid is pumped through porous distributor strips along the leading edges. The pressurisation and air-conditioning system fitted neatly into the unpressurised tailcone. In the nose provision was made for weather radar, but as a customer option (the very first, confidential, brochure suggested the Collins HP-103, whereas a British radar was fitted to the first production aircraft). On the other hand, a British autopilot, the Smiths SEP.2 Type A, was suggested, with the Collins AP-102 as an alternative. An autopilot was deemed essential, unlike the control yoke and pedals for a co-pilot, which, it was thought, should be a customer option.

When Design took over the project the likely engine was the Pratt &

Whitney JT12, with the General Electric CJ610 (J85) and Rolls-Royce RB.145 as possible alternatives. A month into the programme, on 4 June 1960, Dr (later Sir) Stanley Hooker, Technical Director (Aero) of Bristol Siddeley Engines, visited Hatfield determined to sell the 125 team on the Viper. An outstanding and eloquent man, Hooker assured the D.H. men the Viper could do anything the JT12 or CJ610 could do, and committed to a minimum of 2,850 lb thrust. On his return to Bristol he found it needed a fair amount of modification, as explained later,

and the Viper 20 (later called the 520) came out weighing 730 lb compared with the J85's 380! But twelve days later another fine BS engineer, Gordon M. Lewis, reviewed future Viper development for the 125 team and managed to convince them that it was the right way to go. Earlier versions had flown about 200,000 hours in arduous RAF flying training, and in any case de Havilland wanted its engine supplier to be close at hand.

In the course of 1960 the UK's Ministry of Aviation (as it then was)

G-ARYB is seen here with the extended wing span and an anti-spin chute in a tail fairing for stall testing.

reminded the company that there was RAF interest in the D.H.125. It was hinted that, if Hawker Siddeley went ahead and funded the 125 without any help from the government, then support would be forthcoming for the D.H.126 34/36-seat twin-jet feederliner. In the event no such support was ever given, and the 126 was never built, but this did slightly ease the problem facing Wilkins in getting the board to agree to go ahead on the 125. He pulled out all the stops. By starting with the known prices for the components of the Dove and making certain factors and allowances, he arrived at a widely disbelieved selling price for the 125 of £99,950. With this he went to the board and at last, four years after they had first been approached on the 125, the board sanctioned full engineering development on 10 March 1961. It still seemed a bit of a gamble with several million pounds of company money.

In fact, the board agreed that, subject to satisfactory flight testing, an initial production run of 30 aircraft would be committed. What finally clinched the decision was that 20 of these were spoken for by the RAF for use as navigation trainers (Chapter 4). The decision was announced on 6 April, the new aircraft being known as the Jet Dragon. The 30 aircraft were to be built "direct from the design stage", with no prototypes (as had also been the case with the Trident). It was noted that the 125 would "occupy technical staffs who have been responsible for the Comet and Trident jet airliners".

After the decision to go ahead it was not long before the leading departments in the Design Division became involved. On the airframe side, Max Roberts was assigned the wing, Peter Savitsky the fuselage, Jack Dodd flying controls and John Wilson the flight deck. They were supported by the full structural team led by Bob Harper. Aerodynamically the 125 presented a tough challenge, because performance had to be reconciled with simplicity. Wing and stability/control problems were the province of the team led by John Wimpenny, Deputy Chief Aerodynamicist, later Chief Research Engineer. Many aerodynamic solutions were found by Roman Szukiewicz, who had been Assistant Chief Aerodynamicist at Christchurch, and Ron Ashford, later Group Director – Safety Regulations at the Civil Aviation Authority.

As Hatfield was heavily committed to the D.H.121 Trident, production of the 125 was entrusted to the de Havilland factory just outside Chester, which had been one of Britain's most productive aircraft factories during the Second World War. The site had been developed as a "Shadow Factory" by the British Government immediately before war had broken out, and many hundreds of aircraft of differing types were built there. When the war ended the factory was turned over to the production of pre-fabricated buildings, desperately needed in Britain following the devastation caused to many towns and cities by enemy bombing, but de Havilland, pressed for space at Hatfield, bought it in 1948 and it has been a major production plant ever since. Today, as well as producing Hawker 800s and 1000s, it makes the main wing boxes for every version of Airbus, including the massive A330 and A340 structures.

Confusingly, its airfield is called Hawarden (the village of that name being about 2 miles to the west and pronounced Harden), while the factory is actually adjacent to the village of Broughton, immediately to the south. And, while Chester is very much an English city, the Welsh are very proud that the factory and airfield are just inside their border, in the county of Clwyd (pronounced, approximately, to rhyme with "fluid"). So, while the factory is in Wales, it is usually (especially by the English) called "Chester", which is in England....

The entire 125 manufacturing programme was thus assigned to Chester, along with a lot of detail design. Under Chester Chief Engineer Reg Francis, the Project Leader on the 125 was Bob Gurney. Head of the Design Department was Rex Griffiths, who shortly became Chief Engineer. Of course, Hatfield and Chester each thought they were in charge of the 125, and almost everyone involved at either site would, if asked, have said "They think *we* work for *them*".

Predictably a few things changed while the Chester factory was being tooled up to build the 125. The MTO (maximum takeoff) weight, suggested by Wilkins at 17,500 lb, was "about 18,000 lb" in the first press announcement, refined to 18,400 lb in June 1961, and, at exactly the same time, calculated by the Hatfield weight-control staff at 19,300 lb! In the same way, as Wilkins was telling the board that the aircraft could be sold for £99,950, the production staff at both Hatfield and Chester were letting it be known they could not make the parts at the estimated prices, and an even earlier (1960) Project Office estimate came out at "£135,000 to £145,000". The latter proved, in fact, to be a more realistic estimate, and the first aircraft to be sold to a corporate customer was priced in 1964 at £165,000.

Other changes affected the aircraft itself. The first two aircraft, constructor's number (c/n) 25001, with the registration G-ARYA, and 25002, registered G-ARYB, had a wingspan of 44 feet and a short (46 feet 5 inches) body with the main door narrower than in production aircraft. Both pre-production aircraft had their wingspans increased to

47 feet during the development programme. As they were not representative of production aircraft the first two were never sold, but after flight testing ended their days as instructional airframes. They also differed in that they were not completed at Chester but taken by road to Hatfield as soon as the main components had come out of the jigging. As an aside, Jack Garston, Chester General Manager, had been impressed by the vertical jigging pioneered by Tommy Gilbertson at Folland Aircraft, another company taken over by Hawker Siddeley, and he

Following the end of its flying career the second prototype maintained a useful life as an instructional airframe for apprentices in the Hatfield fitting shop. Following the closure of Hatfield in 1993 the airframe was acquired by the Midlands Air Museum at Coventry Airport. With 25001 having been scrapped, G-ARYB is the oldest 125 still in existence.

introduced such jigging at Chester for the 125. Today it is also used for the giant Airbus wings. Such jigging occupies less floor space than the traditional horizontal form of tooling, and facilitates all-round access for the most rapid production.

Components of the first 125 left the Chester plant in March 1962. Assembled, fully equipped and painted at Hatfield, this aircraft made its maiden flight on 13 August 1962, in the hands of test pilot Chris Capper and flight-test engineer Jon Rye, who had previously flown D.H.110 Sea Vixens at Christchurch. Aircraft 'YA was airborne from Hatfield for 56 minutes, and there were no snags. She appeared at the Farnborough Air Show less than a month later, and her sister, 'YB, started flight testing on 12 December 1962. Well before that time it was known that the 125 had been launched into production. ✈

2

The Series 1

From the start of project studies, the de Havilland team had been very conscious of the fact that they were part of a company which, for far longer than any other in the world, had been designing and building commercial jetliners. This inevitably influenced their approach to the 125, which was structurally designed as a jetliner in miniature. This might sound like a mere sales slogan, but numerous customers for the 125 around the world have noticed the difference for themselves. This is not to suggest that any of the competing executive jets are structurally weak or in any other way deficient, but to highlight the exceptional toughness of the 125. For example, most of the wing structure in other business jets is fabricated from sheet, whereas in the 125 the skins and tank end ribs have always been machined from solid billets or plate. An early customer said, "Compared with the —— the 125 is built like a battleship".

The Hatfield team had extensive experience in the matter of structural fatigue. The 125 was designed to ensure that this would never be a problem. Various components were undergoing static and fatigue testing before the first aircraft flew, and a complete fuselage was put through a comprehensive fatigue test programme in a static water tank. Wherever possible the "fail safe" philosophy was adopted, using Redux-bonded doublers and other duplicate load paths, combined with low stress levels throughout. Wherever this philosophy could not be applied, as for example in the main landing gears and engine mountings, unduplicated

parts were designed – usually in high-tensile steel – to have a safe life many times greater than anything the aircraft might accomplish.

As this chapter describes the basic design of the 125 it is largely written in the present tense. Subsequent chapters concentrate on the differences in successive versions. Attention to structure life is seen in the fact that the upper and lower wing skins were designed in one piece but in dissimilar materials. The underskins are a copper-bearing aluminium alloy, noted for its good tension fatigue qualities and slow crack growth. The upper surfaces are of a zinc-bearing alloy. Both skins are stiffened by stringers bonded on by the Redux process, which de

The first four aircraft seen on the ramp at Hatfield.

Havilland pioneered during the Second World War, and which avoids all drilling or other fastening. The wing is assembled as a single structure from tip to tip, the main spar box being sealed with Thiokol to form left and right integral tanks.

The dished centre section is attached to the fuselage by four pairs of machined light-alloy vertical links which pick up the two spars just inboard of the root rib. The left forward links also include a pair of horizontal links to provide lateral bracing. Longitudinal (thrust) forces are transmitted via a single vertical spigot on the centreline at the rear.

The double-slotted flaps extend over 55 per cent of the span. Each is a single unit, pivoted to external hinges of cast aluminium alloy. The two flaps are connected together via torque tubes driven by a single Servodyne hydraulic jack. In the cruise the flaps are housed between upper and lower shrouds. At takeoff they can be set to 15 degrees, and for landing (on early 125s) to the considerable angle of 50 degrees. Just ahead of the mid-portion of each flap are the airbrakes. These take the place of the normal fixed upper and lower flap shrouds. The two upper and two lower brakes are opened by an inching control which balances Servodyne pressure against airstream dynamic pressure, so the brakes can be opened at any speed. The left and right jacks are linked by a cable connection to ensure symmetric operation. The wing leading edges are fixed, and incorporate deicing as described later.

The fuselage is a straightforward cylinder added to an unpressurised tailcone. The skin is copper-bearing aluminium alloy with Reduxed stringers. The skins are jointed at the two wing/fuselage main frames, where there are Reduxed doublers. Technology used in the Trident was adopted for the passenger and cockpit windows. The latter were designed to meet US standards of pilot view and British birdstrike requirements, these being the most severe available. The outermost layer of the multi-laminate windscreens comprises a heat-treated component coated with Triplex GF (gold film) which provides electro-thermal deicing. On each side is a pull-in sliding DV (direct vision) panel. One of the passenger windows on the right side is a pull-in escape hatch, set in a heavy frame with Reduxed doublers.

From the start of flight testing it was only too evident that the 125 was internally noisy, though in the prototype the furnishing and soundproofing were primitive. Later a lead/vinyl sleeve was added around the inside of the cabin, between the fuselage and the trim. Flow breakaway over the top of the cockpit was clearly causing noise and buffet, and in the production aircraft this problem was overcome by adding an unstressed fairing cap over the flight deck, at first aluminium and later honeycomb-filled, with thin lead foil underneath it.

Another change, during the course of the Series 1 production run,

An early view of the production line at Chester. Note the Comets and Sea Vixens in the background.

The intensive US sales tour of 1964 resulted in large numbers of potential customers being exposed to the aircraft. Here Danny Kaye is seen on the flight deck with Mike Kilburn, the Tour Manager.

was to reduce the number of passenger windows from six on each side to five. The forward left-hand window was judged to be not needed, and was omitted to save weight and cost. The corresponding window on the right was omitted when the baggage stowage area was extended rearwards.

In the first two aircraft the main entrance door was rather narrow, but the third 125 was the first built to Series 1 production standard. Among other things the fuselage was lengthened by 12 inches so that the width of the door could be increased to 36 inches. It was designed, like those of the Comet and Trident, to be of the inward-opening plug type. After being pulled in, the door could be swung right up and over to be stowed behind the baggage bay on the right side. A four-step airstairs could then be unfolded from the sill.

In most of the later project studies the tail had been of the T-type. Tunnel testing, combined with the decision to lengthen the forward fuselage, showed the need for greater fin area, and this was added above the horizontal tail.

As previously mentioned, a major modification, retrofitted to the two development aircraft, was the addition of 18 inches to each wingtip and aileron, to improve field performance and provide for future weight growth.

The flight control surfaces are all traditional riveted-sheet structures, with inset hinges and both geared tabs and trim tabs. The elevators and ailerons have forward-projecting tips extending across the tip of the fixed surface to carry mass balances. The cable and pushrod drives are designed to be short enough, combined with a relatively rigid airframe, not to

G-ASNU, the fifth aircraft.

The eighth 125, G-ASSI, bore the brunt of the early demonstration flying completing a demanding tour of North America in November 1964. It returned to Hatfield with 22 sales recorded on its nose by black "kill" silhouettes.

need any length-compensators. Aircraft No 4 was the first to have differential ailerons, subsequently standard.

A unique feature, designed in from the start, is a rudder-bias unit which, following failure of either engine, quickly and automatically applies rudder to keep the aircraft straight. The unit comprises a double-acting pneumatic ram inside the tailcone acting on the large pulley at the base of the rudder post which transmits the pilot control-cable inputs. High pressure bleed air from one engine is fed to one side of the actuator, and bleed air from the other engine to the other side. Thus, with both engines at similar rpm, the ram is centred. Should either engine spool down, the falling bleed-air pressure results in progressive displacement of the ram, and hence of the rudder, almost exactly in proportion to the asymmetry caused by the failed engine.

When the 125 was very young, several crashes of other types of aircraft drew attention to the fact that a rear-engined jet with a T-tail can become locked into a deep stall. During flight development of the 125 nearly 4,000 stalls were carried out to prove that this could never happen to the 125. Nevertheless, to ensure a very positive clean stall the wing leading edges were fitted with triggers (stall strips), immediately outboard of the landing/taxi lights. To contain the stall, modest fences were added above the wing outboard of the triggers, although these were not fitted to the third 125, the Bristol Siddeley aircraft, G-ARYC. Alan Wright,

A rather uninspiring interior of the 1960s.

who had designed the landing gear, was assigned to help solve the 125 development problems.

The Bristol Siddeley Viper 520, as planned for production aircraft, was not certificated until November 1962. The prototypes accordingly began flying with the Mk.511 engine rated at 2,500 lb thrust. In 1963 these were replaced by the standard production engine, the 3,000 lb thrust Mk.520. Apart from being designed to civil airworthiness standards, which required minor changes in material specification, the main change in the Mk.520 was the addition of a zero stage, an extra stage of blading on the front of the compressor. This increased airflow by about 20 per cent and also increased the pressure ratio, the dry weight rising to about 728 lb. The specific fuel consumption, already improved

by the greater pressure ratio, was improved further by reducing turbine entry temperature.

A simple single-shaft turbojet, the Viper was available and fitted in well with the de Havilland philosophy of avoiding complexity. Left and right engines were made identical and neither reversers nor noise suppressers were fitted. Access to the bottom-mounted accessories could be gained while standing on the ground by opening the hinged cowling panels. These aluminium panels could also be quickly detached, allowing three men to change an engine in less than 2 hours.

The landing gear again followed a simple philosophy, for example in the omission of doors over the retracted main wheels (which also enabled tyre width to be increased). Each unit has twin wheels mounted on a single oleo leg of high-strength steel. Nobody would suspect that, to facilitate accommodation of the wheels inside the wing, the axles for the two wheels on each leg are not quite in line. Lockheed Servodyne jacks retract the main units inward into the centre section under the fuselage, and the nose gear forward into a bay with twin doors. Wheels, tyres and Maxaret anti-skid brakes were supplied by Dunlop, with pressure in the main tyres being held to 87 lb/sq in to permit operation from unpaved airstrips. At an early stage the nosewheels were fitted with chined tyres to deflect water and slush sideways, well away from the engines.

Fuel occupies the entire wing box to within 24 inches of the wingtip, total capacity being 1,025 Imp gal (1,231 US gal, 4,660 litres). Left and right tanks are divided into six compartments to prevent surge. When the gravity filler caps in the outer wings are opened, cables pull open flaps to let fuel run down the wing into the centre section, the whole tank being filled in about 10 minutes. Normally the tank booster pumps feed direct to the adjacent engine, but either engine can draw fuel from the entire system. In a steep climb with the tanks nearly empty the booster pumps are isolated, fuel then being drawn by the engine-driven pumps from a rear collector box.

Back in the 1940s de Havilland had stuck its neck out and pressurised the Comet by air bled direct from the engines. The system worked well, and in a refined form was repeated on the 125. Hot air tapped from the last stage of the engine compressors is cooled by passing it through a heat exchanger fed with ram air from the inlet at the front of the dorsal fin extension. A proportion of the cooled air is then refrigerated in a CAU (cold air unit) and the two flows are then remixed according to the temperature selected. The conditioned air passes through a non-return valve in the rear pressure bulkhead and is then divided to flow along an underfloor duct on each side of the cabin. From each duct six pipes take the air up behind the cabin trim to the six outlet "Punkah louvres" which can be adjusted for flow and direction by each passenger. Other pipes warm the pilots' feet and demist the windscreen.

A Kollsman discharge valve in the rear pressure bulkhead maintains pressure differential in the cruise at 8.25 lb/sq in. This corresponds to a cabin altitude of about 6,000 feet at a cruising height of 35,000 feet, and sea-level pressure can be maintained to 21,000 feet altitude.

The butyl rubber seals round the door and emergency exit are inflated to full cabin pressure to ensure perfect sealing, and each of the two Perspex panes of the passenger windows can withstand double the pressurisation load. Should pressure be lost, a Walter Kidde system automatically releases drop-down oxygen masks for all occupants. The 1,400-litre gaseous oxygen bottle is in the nose.

The hydraulic system uses traditional mineral oil. Lockheed fixed-displacement radial pumps driven by each engine draw fluid from a tank in the aft equipment bay, which also has a hand pump for operation on the ground without running the engines. The system operates the flaps, airbrakes, landing gear, nosewheel steering and wheel brakes. In the event of a falling pressure in the system a special valve preserves accumulator pressure for operation of the wheel brakes. There is also a brake accumulator feeding through separate lines. A cockpit handpump is provided for emergency operation of the landing gear and flaps.

Chartag of Switzerland was the first 125 customer, taking delivery of HB-VAG, constructor's number 25006 in September 1964.

Wherever possible seals are duplicated, and many of the components are of proven Comet type. There is not one hydraulic pipe or fuel pipe inside the pressurised fuselage.

Predictably, the electrical system could hardly be simpler. Rotax provided the 28-volt system, using two starter/generators, one on each engine. There is also a static converter as a standby. Raw alternating current for the windscreens is provided by an alternator on the starboard engine.

As briefly mentioned, the leading edges of the wings and tail surfaces are deiced by the TKS system. Fluid is drawn from a 2.5 gallon tank just ahead of the wing under the floor. When selected by the pilot the fluid is pumped along nylon pipes to distributors of porous stainless steel which fit precisely into the profiles of the leading edges. The supply is enough for about one hour of continuous use. The pitot heads and masts are deiced electrically, and the electrically heated windscreen

panels also have an alcohol spray standby system. Hot air from the last compressor stage is used to deice the engine inlets, bullet and guide vanes. Icing is indicated by a Napier sensor projecting from the nose. It senses the increase in torque as ice forms on a splined cylinder which revolves against a cutter.

Should icing cause a pressure buildup in the fuel filters, alcohol is supplied upstream, and this can also be selected by the pilot.

The engine pods are protected against fire by a Graviner Triple FD Firewire detection system, the four zones of each nacelle using sensing elements triggered at different temperatures. The D.H.125 was the first

The fourth 125, G-ASEC, was allocated to the development programme after some use as a demonstrator. One of the tests was to check stone ingestion from the nose wheel, bags being attached to a box latticework fixed to the wing leading edge. Suffice to say the aircraft did not fly in this configuration!

executive type aircraft in the world to be fitted with a "fault free" detection system as original equipment. Each engine is protected by a Graviner extinguisher bottle of the dual-head cartridge-operated type, and either engine can receive two shots of methyl bromide.

By the time the first 125 was flying it seemed likely that most customers would require a dual cockpit (i.e. with control yoke and pedals for both crew members), and this eventually became standard. Another item soon made standard was the Ekco E.190 weather radar, which gave good storm warning out to about 150 miles. Other standard navigation aids included a Marconi ADF (automatic direction finding), with a crossed ferrite antenna under a glassfibre fairing in the top of the fuselage, and a Collins VOR receiver with the antenna near the top of the fin. Collins also supplied the VHF radio(s) and ILS receiver.

At first no decision had been taken on an autopilot. Alan Peters, by then General Manager, despatched Rex Griffiths from Chester, accompanied by Rod Torrington of the Australian Department of Civil Aviation (who were urgently looking at the 125's avionics), to visit the Collins company in Cedar Rapids. Arthur Collins met them personally, and they found their names on the conference room door and even on the blotters and pens inside. But Collins told them he did not think the 125 would find a big market and that he did not wish to bid. Accordingly the fourth aircraft was fitted with an autopilot of a different make, but it proved to be unsatisfactory. When, thus equipped, No 4 went to the 1963 Paris Air Show Hawker Siddeley announced that it was fitted with a Sperry UK autopilot. However soon afterwards Arthur Collins said, "We'll give you two sets, and equip all subsequent 125s". Accordingly the Collins AP-103 autopilot and FD-105 flight director were made standard.

Other equipment includes an Aviquip anti-collision beacon, US General Electric sealed-beam landing and taxi lights grouped in pairs in each wing leading edge, and Avimo airspeed pressure heads mounted on the fuselage. Interior furnishings were left to the customer's choice, as will be apparent throughout the book.

While the first 125 (25001) was used for general handling and development of the systems, the second aircraft was used for performance measurements and the preparation of the operating manual. The third

What the best dressed executive wore in the early 1960s! An early publicity shot.

aircraft, 25003, was a "first" on several counts. It was the first to production standard, and is regarded as the first D.H.125 Series 1. It was the first to be completed and flown at the production factory, at Chester. As noted earlier, it was the only 125 to have no wing fences, and it was the first to be delivered to another operator. Registered G-ARYC, 25003 first flew on 12 February 1963, and after troublefree flight testing was handed over to Bristol Siddeley Engines on 24 July of that year. Initially 'YC was used mainly as a flying testbed for development of the 520-Series Viper, which was still quite a new engine and was being further developed. The immediate objective, of course, was full certification of the engines. After a total of 2,200 hours in 1,660 flights, and prolonged testing on the ground, the 125 achieved its initial objective on 4 June 1964 when the ARB (Air Registration Board, today the Airworthiness Division of the CAA) recommended to the UK

The Plumber's Nightmare. Aircraft number 9 was originally operated by the Civil Aviation Flying Unit (CAFU) as G-ATPC, was acquired by the Royal Aircraft Establishment (RAE) at Bedford in 1970 and allocated the military serial XW930. One of the more unusual programmes allocated to it was the fitting of noise generators above the wing to test the effects of structure in noise shielding. The aircraft actually flew with these generators in place.

Minister of Aviation that the aircraft be granted a Certificate of Airworthiness in the full Air Transport category. This certification was first issued for the eighth aircraft, G-ASSI, on 28 July 1964.

In 1961, before any 125 had flown, de Havilland was visited by Colonel Charles Lindbergh. He was on a mission for PanAm, which was interested in setting up a Business Jets Division, both to operate such aircraft and to act as a US distributor. Discussions went on for almost two years but the stumbling block was that the US airline was really looking for a rather bigger and more sophisticated aircraft.

Although diametrically contrary to the original philosophy of simplicity and value for money the de Havilland Division offered a version with extra fuel and General Electric CF700 aft-fan engines. However they could not guarantee the range and timescale that were being sought and rather reluctantly, in August 1963, PanAm announced selection of a different aircraft.

Of course, Hawker Siddeley's de Havilland Division had to have a demonstrator, representative of the production aircraft, and this need was met by the fourth aircraft, registered G-ASEC and irreverently known at Hatfield as "sausage, egg and chips". This entered service in May 1963, long before certification, and was used for a considerable amount of development flying before taking on its demonstration role. It has since operated all over the world. Like most demonstrators its operations have been varied rather than intensive, and it still had only a modest number of hours when it was re-registered as G-FIVE and operated by Euroair for Group 4 Securities.

G-ARYC was used by Bristol Siddeley (BS) for Viper development and then (when BS became a part of the Rolls-Royce group) was one of the four aircraft used by R-R, notably in support of such collaborative engine programmes as the Olympus 593 for Concorde and RB.199 for the Panavia Tornado. The original BS aircraft was even loaned to the British Concorde partner, British Aircraft Corporation (BAC), on even dates to shuttle staff between the project's two main sites, Bristol and Toulouse in France. In 1967 BAC bought its own 125, which in its first year averaged over 5 hours utilisation a day, carrying an average of 6.9 passengers – an 85 per cent load factor. The author can testify to the fact that those 6.9 people would invariably bring bulging briefcases, huge working drawings, boxes of giant cards for technical briefings, and often such things as big fan blades, hydraulic pumps and avionics boxes!

To demonstrate intensive operation, as well as to accelerate development of the engines, Bristol Siddeley flew its 125 to 16 European capitals in a single day, 7 May 1964. The flight plan of 5,350 miles was flown in just over 14 hours, and a total elapsed time of 19 hours 32 minutes. Today 'YC lives in quiet retirement at the Mosquito Aircraft Museum near Hatfield.

Throughout the flight development of the 125 and the Viper engine,

it was repeatedly demonstrated that, though never intended to be the fastest or longest-ranged business aircraft, the 125 was exceptionally reliable. In particular, flights could be planned to the minute, in the confident expectation that the aircraft would perform precisely as calculated.

This, however, assumes that the captain is familiar with the aircraft. Many of the early customers were pleasantly surprised to find that cruising speeds were in general slightly up on those promised, and fuel burns markedly less. In some cases the improvement was remarkable, as related later.

The first 125 delivered to a customer was 25006. Registered HB-VAG, it was handed over on 2 September 1964 to Chartag of Zurich. The first of two for the Swiss charter operator, priced at £165,000 each, its livery was a white top with red cheat line and fin. It was abundantly equipped with communications radios, including twin "towel rail" ADF sense antennas along the top of the fuselage. (The first 125 to have such an antenna had been the Bristol Siddeley aircraft, which had the more usual single rail.)

Several other early sales were achieved in Europe, but it was self-evident that by far the biggest market was to be found in North America. In 1964 the United States alone had approximately 35,000 business and executive aircraft, far more than the rest of the world put together. Accordingly, the company demonstrator G-ASSI (always called "Gassy") departed on 7 August 1964, less than two weeks after its maiden flight, on a tour of North America. It was one of the most extensive sales tours ever, flown by Mike Maina, the 125 demonstration pilot who later joined Bowater, and former D.H .Propellers Chief Test Pilot, Mike Kilburn.

When 'SI returned to Hatfield on 15 November it had flown, according to several American observers, "more than the average executive aircraft flies in a year". It had logged well over 500 hours in 105 days, making 554 flights and visiting 105 airfields (some several times) in 32 US states and six Canadian provinces. It was flown by 300 pilots, not one of whom was unimpressed.

The immediate result was 20 orders, in addition to two taken previously. Equally significant, a North American dealership was established, and the groundwork was laid for continued sales in the biggest, and toughest, market in the world. But these sales were for improved aircraft. Only eight Series 1 aircraft were built. It was largely the crucial importance of being as competitive as possible that led to such an early introduction of improvements.

In spite of being named Jet Dragon at the start of development, the 125 was never marketed as such, the decision to drop the name being made at a board meeting in August 1961. One reason was that the US market was used to numerical designations. Another was that a company humorist kept saying the 125 would have "a jet draggin' along the ground". How could the name survive that?

3
Improved Series 1s

From a distance of over 30 years it is difficult to track down "who did what". However this is an appropriate point at which to name more of the top designers. R.E. Bishop, the Technical Director, had ceased to be an active designer by the end of 1960, leaving Tim Wilkins as Chief Designer at Hatfield, with J.P. (Phil) Smith and Alan Peters as deputies. When Joe Goodwin went to Grumman in 1964 he was replaced by Bill Tamblin's deputy, Ron Gilbert. About 18 months later he was in turn replaced briefly by Tamblin himself, and then by Peter Cedervall, who saw the 125 right through to the Series 800. Cedervall was supported initially by Peter Stalkartt and subsequently by Max Roberts, as explained in Chapter 7.

It was known from the start that the United States would not only be by far the biggest market but also the most competitive. For a foreign manufacturer to sell successfully into this giant market, spares support has to be at least as good as that offered by domestic manufacturers. Many often bitter lessons were learned in the early days with the Dove, and de Havilland was determined to do it right with the 125 from the outset. The high standard of product support offered with the 125 from Day One unquestionably made a large contribution to its continued sales success throughout North America. Technical representatives came under Ron Godfrey at Hatfield and Ian Farquarson-Keith in the United States. Another key man at Hatfield was Peter Mitchell, who completed a 25-year involvement with the 125 as Sales Manager in 1986.

In autumn 1963, very soon after PanAm pulled out, North American distributors were appointed. They were Atlantic Aviation Sales Corporation, of Wilmington, Delaware; AiResearch Aviation Services, of Los Angeles; and Timmins Aviation (later Atlantic Aviation of Canada and later still Innotech), of Montreal. Fossett had for years recognised them as market leaders in the business of installing sophisticated avionics and plush executive interiors. He wanted the best for the 125.

Following the eight Series 1 aircraft, all production was divided into two streams, called A (America) and B (rest of world). The first of these was aircraft 25013, delivered to Atlantic Aviation in September 1964. At the same time the designation was changed from D.H.125 to Hawker

An early specially configured 125 was aircraft number 15, used by the Australian DCA for the calibration of navigation aids. As a result, there were only four windows on the starboard side to allow for the housing of the extra equipment.

Siddeley HS 125, though in the United States the name de Havilland was better known and to a considerable degree continued to be used by the distributors and customers. For this market the aircraft were designated D.H.125 Series 1A. These were completed at Chester as "green" aircraft, totally unfurnished and externally unpainted. For the long delivery flight they would be equipped with the minimum essential avionics, carried on board in a crate. The ferry pilots often too had to carry on board an old wooden box with a piece of string attached, with which it could be lowered from the door to the ground to take the place of proper airstairs. The crates of radio equipment and the wooden box were destined to make many dozens of Atlantic crossings.

Arriving at Wilmington or Los Angeles the nondescript 125 would, over a period of a few weeks, be completely transformed. It would emerge with the interior furnishings, avionics and external paint scheme required by the customer. The system worked well. With an executive jet, even one as keenly priced as a 125, the customer (represented variously by the Chairman of the Board, the Chief Pilot or a senior ground engineer, if the company did its own maintenance) almost always wishes to pay

frequent visits to see how the completion process is progressing. Use of local distributors enormously facilitated this essential and ideally intimate process.

Aircraft for the rest of the world were designated HS 125 Series 1B, and these were completed at Chester. They also differed slightly from the Series 1A aircraft, as described later. Improvements to all Series 1s included greater power, an improved structure and increased gross weights. Bristol Siddeley found that the zero-stage on the Viper compressor enabled the engine to be progressively uprated above the initial 3,000 lb. Deliveries in 1965 were of the Viper 521, rated at 3,120lb under ISA (International Standard Atmosphere) conditions, but flat-

Atlantic Aviation was one of the distributors appointed in North America in 1963. It received its first aircraft in September 1964.

rated to maintain power under hot or high-altitude conditions. At 5,000 feet and 30°C, for example, the increase in thrust over the Mk.520 was 530 lb, which could mean either more payload or an extra 120 miles in range. This engine began life with a TBO (time between overhauls) of 800 hours, and with the unusual advantage of a "power by the hour" deal under the terms of which Bristol Siddeley undertook to carry out all overhauls, parts-life rectification and modification for a price of £7.75 per flown hour.

Among the airframe improvements in the 1A and 1B were a lighter wing structure (despite the clearance to higher gross weights) and a number of local modifications to reduce drag, the most important being more extensive use of flush riveting. Maximum takeoff (MTO) weight of the Series 1B was increased. For example, whereas the Series 1 would carry 800 lb for 1,100 nautical miles, the 1B could carry 1,700 lb for 1,280 nautical miles, one of the biggest single increases in the whole 125 story. On the other hand the Series 1A, subject to US Federal Aviation Agency (FAA) regulations, had to be restricted to a takeoff weight of 20,500 lb, because MTO weight is not allowed to exceed 105 per cent of MLW (maximum landing weight) without a fuel-jettison system, which back in 1960 de Havilland had had been eager to avoid.

A Series 1A-521, belonging to American Management Association, is seen over New York.

This was the first Series 1B-522 and is seen here in an early publicity shot. The aircraft belonged to Mines Air Services of Zambia.

Shell Aircraft receives its first 125 in 1966. The line-up includes: Peter de Havilland, son of Sir Geoffrey, (second from left); Sir Douglas Bader (second from right); and Alan Peters, Deputy Chief Designer, (right).

The principal differences between the 1A and 1B were concerned with systems, equipment and avionics. For example, 'B' aircraft retained the HSD (Hawker Siddeley Dynamics) air-conditioning system, whereas 'A' aircraft used an AiResearch system. From the 100th aircraft, the main electrical system has a split (instead of single) busbar. 'A' aircraft increasingly used US radio and navigation aids, including the radar. For various technical and marketing reasons the US content of the 125 was to rise progressively over the next 25 years.

Bristol Siddeley continued to develop the Viper, and from October 1965 the HS 125 was fitted with the Mk.522 engine. This was first flown in the engine development aircraft G-ASEC, the second production 125, in November 1964. It incorporated numerous aerodynamic modifications and as a result thrust was increased to 3,360 lb, and maintained either to 21°C or to 3,000 feet. This made a big difference to takeoff field length, and on an airfield at 5,000 feet at 30°C the MTO weight could be increased from 17,500 lb to 19,500 lb! Indeed, the improvement in takeoff distance caused Hawker Siddeley to look carefully at the use of larger wheels with low-pressure tyres for really soft airstrips.

The first production aircraft with the new engine was 25062, the first of two HS 125s for Qantas (which were actually Series 3Bs as described later), for use as crew trainers. Early in 1966 it was all ready for delivery but on its acceptance flight a turbine blade came through the fuselage. This was precisely the sort of thing that was not supposed to happen with a 125, and Bristol Siddeley responded with urgency. As an immediate interim cure the company drilled each turbine blade and laced them all together with a ring of wire to damp vibration. The resulting penalty in performance was accepted for just over a year until the Viper engineers, by now employees of Rolls-Royce, which bought Bristol Siddeley in October 1966, had perfected a solution to the problem. Aircraft 25062, fitted with Mk.522 engines, was delivered to Qantas, along with 25069, but what might not have been expected was that by 1982 it had made 53,882 landings with the Australian airline. It was last heard of lying in a field outside Sydney, but there are rumours that it is to be brought back to flying condition again.

In early 1965 the Hatfield team urgently worked on a completely new 125 variant. As it was for military use, responsibility for the project was later passed to Hawker Siddeley's Brough factory, on the east coast of England, which was one of the company's "military" sites. Known as the Alternative Roles Aircraft, it was to be used mainly as a naval courier (communications), which required no major change, and as an AEW (airborne early warning) platform, which required considerable redesign. The main electronic contractor, Elliott Bros., (now a part of GEC Avionics) proposed fitting a radar antenna housed in a rotodome carried above the fuselage, there being two possible antenna sizes with diameters of 12.75 feet and 16 feet. A twin-finned tail (vertical stabiliser) was also necessary. This aircraft could also be used for ASW (anti-submarine warfare), transport, ambulance, training and other missions. It never got off the drawing board, but today multirole military Hawkers, under

Aircraft 94 was the one and only Series 1B/R-522 fitted with a long-range tank.

the generic term Special Variants, are in production and represent an important and significant part of the company's business.

In November 1965 Series 1A c/n 25036, registered CF-PQG, was delivered as the flagship of the fleet of aircraft operated by the Département de Transports et Communications of the Government of Quebec, Canada. In its first 30 days it flew over 100 hours carrying 331 passengers on 80 missions. This was despite the fact that, in the words of Air Service Director Paul Gagnon, "We had every possible type of precipitation – rain, snow, freezing rain, snow grains, ice pellets, sleet and hail. Eighty per cent of our flights were carried out from runways covered with ice, slush or snow, and 75 per cent of our landings and takeoffs were under instrument weather conditions". The aircraft clearly thrived on such treatment, because ten years later it had become the second 125 to exceed 10,000 hours, with almost 13,000 landings. It had been used for VIP missions and every kind of emergency including ambulance services.

By 1966 the price of a 125 had firmly begun to climb, but it still remained extremely competitive. Predictably, the 1960 estimate of

£100,000 proved to be a pious hope, and, as already mentioned, the first customer, Chartag, paid £165,000. By 1965 a Series 1B with Mk.522 engines was priced, with a standard six-seat interior but without radio, at £228,000. Avionics and a more lavish interior might add a further £60,000.

Figures for a Series 1A are less easy to quote, because the standard of build varied so widely. In general, aircraft for the US market were more fully equipped than the Series 1Bs (though there were many exceptions), an important extra being an AiResearch GTP-3O APU (auxiliary power unit) in the tailcone. The APU, which by the 1960s was an expected feature in a US executive aircraft, could provide electric power on the ground but was used primarily to keep the cabin at a comfortable temperature no matter whether the airport was at 40°C or -40°C. A typical US price for a fully equipped Series 1A in the winter of 1966-67 was fractionally over $1 million, of which $250,000 was down to the US distributor and the equipment he installed.

Perhaps the most colourful 125 ever built was an early 1B supplied to Kwame Nkrumah, the flamboyant President of Ghana – a state which he virtually created from the former British colony, the Gold Coast. Though nominally belonging to the Air Force it was a riot of pinks, blues and anodised gold. The aft bulkhead was a gigantic picture of – guess who? Unfortunately for him, his profligacy resulted in his deposition in 1966, but at least he escaped with his life. Not so another African President, Moise Tshombe, head of the Congolese breakaway province of Katanga. In 1965 he was condemned to death *in absentia*, and two years later his chartered 125 Series 1B was the subject of a bloody hijack which, among other things, left the 125 riddled with holes

▲ *Early interior designs were fairly utilitarian by today's standards.*

and the innocent British crew in jail in Algiers – where they might still be today had it not been for the efforts of the pilot's father and the Red Cross.

An early customer for a Series 1B was the French industrialist Roland Fraissinet, whose companies and affiliates include Transair, who represented Hawker Siddeley in France. Fraissinet very frequently flew 125s of Transair's subsidiary Air Affaires, and at the start of 1966 he demonstrated the type's STOL (short takeoff and landing) performance from the 2,920-foot grass runway at Cannes. With 561 gallons of fuel, sufficient to fly to London, the 125 positively leapt into the air 1,600 feet from brakes-release. Two hours later Fraissinet landed, coming to a stop in 1,700 feet. The surface wind, the records tell us, was just 6 knots at around 50 degrees to the runway.

In September 1966 G.D.P. Worthington and R. Earp-Jones flew VQ-ZIL, owned by the Swaziland Iron Ore Development Corporation, from Hatfield to Johannesburg. Despite some fierce weather, an active bush fire on the approach and other hazards, the trip was a textbook example of 125-1B operation. Worthington commented, "We made our first fuel check just west of Southampton at 35,000 feet and found that we had used 100 lb less than we had allowed for". The whole trip took 17 hours 39 minutes flight time, flown in nine sectors. (Today a Hawker 1000 could do it with one stop!) But almost every early customer reported that fuel burn was below prediction.

A slightly unusual US customer was Blount Brothers, a heavy construction contractor which in 21 years had grown from nothing to a $175 million annual business. W.M. Blount, the President, not only obtained his Type Rating on the 125 but went to Chester to collect his firm's 125-1A ("green" of course, totally unfurnished) and flew it across the Atlantic to Greater Wilmington airport where he delivered it to Atlantic Aviation for completion to his requirements!

Today the giant Bowater organisation uses several aircraft, but its very first was N2125, a 125 delivered in July 1966. This was normally based at Newark, New Jersey, with most trips following an established route structure to Montreal, Nova Scotia and Newfoundland to the north, and to Chattanooga, Atlanta and Charlotte to the south. But each spring and autumn 2125 was taken to McAlpine Aviation's base at

Passing 100...

The 100th 125, a Series 1A-522 for the US market, rolled off the Chester production line on Friday, 15 July 1966. At that time the average production rate was seven aircraft a month, and 52 125s had been delivered to the USA.

Luton, England, in order to spend some weeks serving Bowater's interests throughout Europe.

For one aircraft to serve both the US and European regions was unheard of in 1966. Another unusual customer was the Banco Nacional de Mexico. A long-time operator of first a Dove and then a D.H.114 Heron, the bank received its 125-1A in January 1966. Champagne flowed, and unlike many customers the bank was not only proud to publicise its new acquisition but even to report on its performance and costs. This 125 seldom had to cope with bad weather, but always had the problem of the very hot thin air at airfields some 7,000 feet above sea level (Mexico City airport is at 7,340 feet elevation.).

Some of the early aircraft became visibly different as they undertook special research programmes. One of the first aircraft, number 25009, was completed as a Series 1B, with the civil registration G-ATPC, but was sold in 1971 to what was then the Royal Aircraft Establishment (RAE), bearing the UK military registration XW930. Based at the RAE research airfield at Thurleigh near Bedford, it quickly proved ideal in programmes of gust research, noise and the use of a laser to measure true airspeed. In the extensive noise programme it spent some time with a standard Viper 520 on the right side but a Viper 601 on the left, fitted with a massive tandem arrangement of an eight-lobe silencing nozzle and a giant ejector nozzle. Later it was fitted with an array of prominent external pipes leading to noise generators in various parts of the aircraft, producing tones which were distinguishable from engine noise. One subject of these tests was to assess the importance of having engines shielded from the ground by part of the airframe. This amazing configuration led to at least one wag calling it "the plumber's nightmare".

As a research aircraft with the RAE, aircraft 25009 actually became something of a "Jack-of-all-trades". Among the many other tasks assigned to it was investigation into windshear and microbursts; a joint programme with NASA looking at the use of satellites in weather forecasting; research into Terrain Following Radar; wake turbulence and storm turbulence investigations; and, in the mid-1980s, trials for the Ferranti Blue Vixen

radar system, carried out in the company of a Series 600, which are recorded in more detail in Chapter 7.

There is no better way of concluding this chapter than to quote the Chief Pilot of an Ohio paper company which was the very first US customer.

"So far this month, our second of operation, there have been only three days the aircraft has not been scheduled for a flight, and there were very few more in the first 30 days

"To date, we have not experienced a single delay or cancellation due to aircraft or engine malfunction – in fact none for any reason. The problems that have occurred have all been minor and not 'no go' items. In the case of the one aircraft part malfunction (the nose-steering valve) we were able to continue operation, using brakes for steering, until the new valve was installed. Incidentally, the delivery service on this part was very good; it was received on the same day that it was ordered.

"The performance and operation in every way exceeds the claims and guarantees and our own projections. In the first month's operation our average ground-to-ground speed (start of takeoff roll to landing touchdown) was 380 mph. True airspeed at 27,000-28,000 feet in ISA conditions has averaged 505 mph, and never less than 495 mph. Fuel used from start-up to cruise altitudes of 35,000-37,000 feet has averaged 1,200 lb and usually is 200-400 lb less than the factory specifications.

"In our current second month of operation, we have already accumulated 48 hours. The total landings to date are 105, all on the original tyres which still show tread. All operations are still on-time, with no cancellations for malfunctions. All in all, a most impressive record of dependability for any aircraft, and especially for a new jet aircraft. Truly, the D.H.125 is far exceeding our expectations, which is most pleasing to those of us in operations. Our management people are also well satisfied that picking the D.H.125 was a wise decision.

"It is my firm belief that the D.H.125 will become as well known a 'workhorse' as the DC-3, with many, many more pluses!" ✈

4

The Series 2: Dominie

Britain's Royal Air Force has a history of tight budgets, and repeatedly it has been unable to fund equipment that is urgently, and even obviously, needed. Thanks to the 125 it has been able to plug at least one major gap in its aircraft inventory: navigation training for those who will later fly as navigators in fast jets.

Back in the 1950s the service had a choice of two aircraft for this task. One was the Vickers-Armstrongs Varsity T.1 which, with a few rather similar Valetta T.3s, was really a "flying classroom". One of its drawbacks was that its piston engines gave it a cruising speed of only about 180 knots. The other type was the Gloster (Armstrong Whitworth) Meteor NF(T).14. Though a fast jet, able to cruise at 450 knots, it was a conversion of a night fighter. It had just two seats, the rear one quite a long way behind the pilot. There was no room for many of the essential tools a navigator used in the 1960 era, nor for an instructor, and all the NF(T).14 could really do was give pupils a taste of high-speed flying and possibly some experience in fast map-reading.

Obviously there was a need for a new aircraft, combining jet performance with the ability to carry all necessary navigation aids plus pupils and an instructor. There has been much debate on how many student navigators should be accommodated. Back in the Second World War one of the most famous de Havilland products, the D.H.89 Dragon Rapide, a twin-engined biplane, had appeared as a navigation trainer. It had been given the name "Dominie" (a Scottish term for a schoolmaster, and also, in the USA, a clergyman). Though only a small aircraft, with just 400 horse power, the Dominie trained six pupils at a time, though at that time of course without needing modern navigation aids. In the US Air Force the "classroom" philosophy has persisted to this day. The standard aircraft is the T-43A, a version of the Boeing 737-200 with 19 navigator stations in its capacious fuselage – twelve for undergraduate navigators, four for advanced students and three for instructors. Had the RAF adhered to this philosophy it would probably have ended up with a fleet of BAC One-Eleven jetliners.

In contrast, by 1960 the RAF had firmly come to the opinion that the optimum number of student navigators was two. It had been well pleased with the arrangement in the Varsity where the rear of the cabin, aft of the wing spar, was occupied by two trainee navigators, seated side-by-side, facing aft at a console on the rear bulkhead and overseen by a navigation instructor. It was found that the one-plus-two arrangement enabled the instructor to maintain watch on both students, to give individual tuition and to let either student have complete responsibility for actually navigating the aircraft.

What the RAF was resigned to was not having the money to fund an aircraft designed to its own requirements. Nevertheless, in 1960 it issued an ASR (Air Staff Requirement) and was immediately intrigued to learn of the interest at Hatfield in building a "jet-propelled Dove replacement". This sounded like precisely the aircraft the RAF was seeking, and discussions quickly confirmed this. It was soon established that the D.H.125 would not need any significant modification to meet the RAF's requirement, other than a custom-built interior and a special suite of

The Dominie Navigation Trainer for the RAF originally flew in overall silver colours with dayglo patches on the nose, tail and wing tips. The RAF order for 20 aircraft used up a major part of the initial production batch of 30 aircraft allowing early deliveries of the improved Series 1A and 1B.

Before entering service with the RAF, the Dominies were painted in a new grey, red and white scheme, introducing these colours to the Training Command fleet.

avionics.

In particular, the RAF went along totally with the basic de Havilland philosophy of sacrificing some performance, and to some degree appearance, in order to achieve low price, economical operation, the longest possible fatigue-free life and, not least, the highest possible reliability. Air Chief Marshal Sir Thomas Pike, at that time Chief of the Air Staff, told the author, "If we had had it designed to our requirements I don't think one rivet would have been changed".

Selling executive jets always has a certain air of uncertainty about it. Long knives in the boardroom can result in new faces who don't want the aircraft, and even getting customers actually to pay can sometimes be difficult. In contrast, the UK Ministry of Defence was a known quantity, and the fact that the RAF had a requirement for 20 aircraft played a crucial role in securing a go-ahead for the 125 programme. An order from the RAF would comprise two-thirds of the initial commitment to build 30 aircraft. It would also allow 20 of the first 30, heavier, Series

1 aircraft to be diverted to the RAF and thus make early production Series 1A and 1B aircraft available for civil use.

Contract negotiations with the MoD started in September 1962, shortly after the maiden flight of the first 125, with the contract finally being awarded in April 1964. Repeating the name of the wartime biplane, the RAF called its new trainer, which is technically a 125 Series 2, the Dominie T.1. Development of this variant took place in the closest collaboration with the RAF, and the first Dominie flew in December 1964. Deliveries continued until August 1966. The Dominie entered service in December 1965 with No 1 ANS (Air Navigation School) at Stradishall, Suffolk, with the first Dominie-trained course of navigators passing out in April 1966.

The airframe of the Dominie is virtually identical to that of the original 125 Series 1, though the engines, designated Viper Mk.301, are rated at 3,000 lb and are equivalent to the civil Mk.520. The cabin has six windows on the port (left) side, but the two forward starboard windows are omitted because of the electronic equipment racks. The only unusual external feature is that the wing/body fairing, from the start a prominent

Part of the student console at the rear of the Dominie cabin. The RAF liked basics.

feature on the 125, was extended forward under the fuselage ahead of the wing. This, together with other minor changes in appearance, compared with civil 125s, was because of the special fit of electronic navigation aids – in particular a doppler radar and different communications. The extended fairing required the addition of a ventral fin at the tail.

Like other early Series 1 aircraft, the Dominie T.1 has an up-and-over plug door. This slides round the top of the cabin, but instead of coming to rest behind the baggage it lies above and behind the toilet, which is opposite the entrance, with the Lox (liquid oxygen) pack beside it. Civil 125s use gaseous oxygen. The RAF decided not to pay for inbuilt airstairs, so the Dominie requires a small flight of steps to be wheeled up to it for access.

The main cabin could have been arranged for an instructor and three pupils, but the RAF adhered to its policy of training just two undergraduates (to use the US term) at a time. They sit in fixed rearward-facing seats at a console occupying the entire upper part of the rear of the cabin. This console comprises a horizontal chart table with a vertical bank of traditional instruments beyond. In the centre of the cabin is a small seat for the operator of a periscopic sextant. This seat has unobstructed access all round, swivels through 360 degrees, and is located approximately on the aircraft CG (centre of gravity) to minimise acceleration errors. On the left side are two further aft-facing seats, one for the instructor to overlook the pupils and the other, next to the door, being available for a supernumerary crew member or passenger.

It has always been RAF policy to give aircrew a thorough grounding in whatever subject is being taught, even if the particular technique has passed into history. Thus, the Dominie was equipped for map reading, maintaining a dead-reckoning plot on a chart with pencil and drawing instruments, taking sights with a sextant and use of the Decca Navigator. To be fair, most of these long-established techniques were used by navigators of the V-bombers, which were still very much in service in the mid-1960s.

The communications fit of the Dominie likewise paralleled that in many RAF front-line aircraft, namely duplicate HF, VHF, and UHF radios. In early civil 125s, if HF was fitted, it used an external "towel rail" antenna above the fuselage, but in the Dominie the HF antenna is a suppressed notch cutout in the dorsal fin.

The RAF was insistent on its requirements for intercom. As a result the system provides selection and mixing of all audio services between the pilots, the staff navigator and the students. Either pupil has to be able to talk to the pilot(s), for example to give courses to steer and other navigation instructions, but with the staff navigator listening. Alternatively, the staff (instructor) navigator has to be able to talk to either pupil, without the other pupil being able to hear, as well as being able to address both simultaneously.

Unlike civil 125s there is no weather radar display in the cockpit. This, together with the radar controls, was moved to the students' console. The Decca Type 62 doppler radar is the reason for the extended belly fairing. This has a plate antenna under the forward fuselage, housed in the glassfibre fairing, and feeds drift, groundspeed and distance gone to displays on the students' console.

The master gyro platform is installed on the centreline under the students' plotting table. The compass feeds displays for the captain (left-hand pilot) and first student. Another navigation aid is the GPI (ground-position indicator). This is fed with information from the gyro-magnetic compass and from the doppler, plus certain data added by either student, and outputs geographical position in terms of latitude/longitude co-ordinates. There are two GPIs, one for each student. The captain and first student both have an RMS (radial magnetic selector) for flying VOR radials. Only the pilot has ILS, giving a standard crossed-needle

The RAF College at Cranwell operated some Dominies for a while, until they all joined 6FTS at Finningley. With the closure of Finningley the Dominies are to return to Cranwell.

display. The avionics fit is completed by the autopilot and IFF (identification friend or foe, or SSR transponder).

When the Dominie entered service with No 1 ANS, to which was soon added the RAF College of Air Warfare at Manby in Lincolnshire, many RAF missions were still flown at high altitude. At first the Dominie handled the "fast and high" training, the "low and slow" tuition being assigned to Varsities. From 1970, however, the RAF progressively concentrated all fixed-wing training for aircrew other than pilots at 6 FTS (Flying Training School) at Finningley in Yorkshire. Originally featuring a black nose radome, fluorescent red nose and tail and otherwise silver fuselage, the Dominies introduced what became standard RAF training colours of a white top and unpainted underside separated by a wide red cheatline. The radome is white, and ahead of the cockpit is a black anti-dazzle panel. The vertical tail is white, but each aircraft bears its individual letter on a red stripe above the serial number.

Most 125s, including Dominies, have had relatively uneventful careers. Unlike pilot training, navigator training seldom puts the aircraft in unnatural or dangerous attitudes, and the only really untoward thing that ever happened to a Dominie was when one suffered hydraulic failure while on the approach. The co-pilot unstrapped the emergency hydraulic handpump handle, but the Dominie nevertheless arrived smoothly on its belly. It was found that the unfortunate crew-member had been furiously "pumping" the rudder-pedal locking mechanism.

For many years navigators have flown an 85-hour course in the Dominie, with AEOs (air electronics officers) completing 48 hours. Again for many years, virtually all RAF front-line combat missions have been undertaken at low level, so though tanker and transport aircrew need traditional skills, backseaters in fast jets have to "hack it" at treetop height. Part of the arduous task of navigator training is handled by Finningley's Dominies in the LLTS (Low-Level Training Squadron). This subjects the aircraft to much harsher treatment than any civil 125s receive, with high speed at low level for about 600 hours annually.

Despite this, the tough airframe of the basic 125 just keeps on flying without cracks appearing, and in 1996, 30 years after entering service eleven Dominies are undergoing a major conversion to fit them for service well into the 21st century. When the Dominie entered service the most important single task was to train navigators for V-bombers. They faced

The first (Trial Installation) Dominie T.Mk.2, XS728. The modified aircraft are distinguished by the windows on the port side and the slightly extended (12 inches) nose radome.

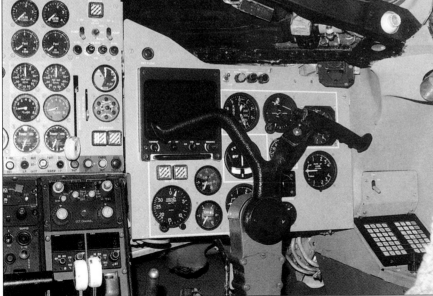

Three views of the cabin of the Dominie T. Mk. 2. Top left, the second navigator/ instructor console; bottom left, the right hand seat console (co-pilot's seat); and above, the master navigation console.

to the rear, and used a mapping radar and other equipment which by modern standards was primitive, and often merely an updated version of that used in the Second World War. The advent of the Buccaneer and Tornado required modern avionics used by a two-man crew employing totally different procedures and techniques. The Dominie took in its stride the new requirement of low-level training, but its equipment was entirely unsuited to the changed training task.

Accordingly, in 1991 the Air Staff issued a requirement for a major update, to fit eleven of the surviving 19 aircraft to the training demand until at least the year 2015. Following a competition the prime contract was awarded to Thorn EMI Electronics, with Marshall Aerospace undertaking all aircraft redesign, refurbishment, modification and flight test. Key features include a completely new integrated digital navigation system and a modern radar with nose-mounted scanner. The modified aircraft are designated Dominie T.Mk.2 in RAF service.

The system's conceptual design predictably reflects the RAF's wish to minimise price and risk, so almost every item is based on off-the-shelf equipment. The radar is the Thorn Super Searcher, with the performance and picture quality to give good ground mapping at all heights, and with aircraft speed matched to range scale and picture resolution. Its 3-axis scanner is mounted in the nose to obtain a good picture at high angles of bank. The nose is 12 inches longer, but no change to the fin was needed. The radar feeds through a powerful Thorn RNPU (radar navigation processing unit), which interfaces with and provides operating controls for the subsystems.

Navigation sensors include a Sperry GM Mk 7A compass, Racal 72RB Doppler and Penny & Giles Digitas air-data computer. The cockpit has Rockwell Collins Pro Line II digital avionics, with dual VOR-32, dual DME-42, ADF-462 and Tacan TCN-500.

Marshall Aerospace gutted each cabin and re-equipped it for a crew of six, of whom three are navigators under training, all facing forwards. The MNC (master navigation console) is the prime student station on the right of the cabin. The RHSC (right-hand seat console) is the copilot station in the cockpit. The SNIC (second navigator/instructor console) is on the left. At the rear of the cabin is a station for an AEO. There is also a seat for a student waiting to move to one of the training stations, as well as two "perch seats" for passengers or observers. All stations are linked by an improved and extended intercom system.

The entire system has been planned for future adaptability and growth. Throughout, there is extensive BITE (built-in test equipment). Racal Radar Defence Systems (which took over the radar activities of Thorn EMI Electronics in 1995) and Marshall are responsible for relevant publications, and for supporting the aircraft in service. The contracts were divided into a single T1 (trial installation) aircraft, and for work on the subsequent ten aircraft. Marshall collected the Dominies from RAF Finningley, and began work on the T1 aircraft (XS728) at Cambridge in July 1992. Since then the Dominie squadron has become part of No. 3 Flying Training School and has been relocated to RAF Cranwell. Work on upgrading the last four aircraft was underway as this book went to print, and the final aircraft is due for delivery by the end of 1996. ✈

5

The Series 3 and 3RA

By 1965 the Hawker Siddeley 125 had very much arrived on the world scene, and it had repeatedly shown its ability to compete strongly. The original Hatfield design philosophy could be seen by this time to be a two-edged weapon. A keen selling price was important to many customers, but an even greater number were prepared to pay more to get greater capability. In the matters of size, field length and general cruising performance the 125 was hard to fault, and its toughness and reliability were taken for granted. Some customers found the aircraft somewhat marginal in its range and in some of the systems and equipment fitted.

Increasing range tends to mean a bigger and more expensive aircraft. In designing the aircraft one has to contend with a vicious spiral (some engineers would say there are several) which multiplies the problems. More fuel means a bigger aircraft, which means the need for more engine power, which means more rapid fuel burn, and so on. To obtain even a range extension of 20 per cent can have awesome consequences in weights and costs, and also tends to mean that the aircraft needs much longer runways. Without wishing to rush too many fences at once, the overall story of the 125 is almost beyond belief; today's versions can fly missions absolutely undreamed of 25 years ago.

To give a flavour for the thinking at the time 125 was launched, the following appeared in the British technical magazine *Aircraft Engineering* in its issue of February 1963: "It is rather difficult to choose the right maximum range for a business aircraft. The average flight length of those currently in use is very short, sometimes between 100 and 200 miles. These aircraft are, however, propeller-driven, relatively slow and noisy; both of which characteristics tend towards the selection of short duration flights, whereas the D.H.125, faster and aiming at a higher level of comfort, could well make long stages more popular. In the end, a full-reserves range (at full payload) of at least 1,100 nautical miles was aimed for....." At about this time John Scott, Martin Sharp's successor as PR Manager at Hatfield, told the author, "The indications are that flights as long as 1,000 miles will be very much the exception".

That may well have been true in the case of most customers, but the 125 designers had to keep on responding to the largest market, the United States. Here the need for not just a little more range but a lot more range, was becoming insistent. It was just as tough on Hawker Siddeley's rivals, but the 125 designers spent 1965 urgently studying

what could be done. Some of the options were fairly simple, and some were very major changes demanding quite a long timescale. For the immediate future, for deliveries starting from the end of 1966, the Series 3A and 3B were introduced. The US distributors and customers were rather disappointed that this had unchanged fuel capacity. In many other respects it represented a significant advance on the 1A/1B.

The Series 3 was made possible by the Viper 522 engine, which, with an average takeoff rating of 3,360 lb, gave useful performance improvements *(see Appendix 3)*.

Where the Series 3 did mark a real advance was in its systems. Over the long life of the 125, several of the items of British equipment have been replaced by items from the United States. The makers have always been concerned to furnish their customers with the best possible product, and in a competitive world this has inevitably meant changing many of the sources. The process really began with the Series 3, where Hawker

The first of the two Series 3Bs for Qantas, VH-ECE, broke all records for high flight hours and landings.

The early 125s did not have the main undercarriage fully enclosed. This underside view of the Fabbri 125-2B also shows the central skid for protection in the event of a wheels up landing.

Used as a development aircraft for the longer range 125 3B/RA, aircraft 25094, G-ATWH, was fitted with a ventral fuel tank. For stall tests a tail spin parachute was also installed in a fairing under the rudder.

Siddeley threw out its own pressurisation and air-conditioning system and replaced it with an AiResearch installation. This Los Angeles-based company, already the 125 US West Coast distributor, had enormous experience with small turbo-machinery, and its system was lighter, less bulky and more efficient thermodynamically. It facilitated the addition of the same company's APU, which was already virtually standard on 125s for the US market. It was offered as an option on the 3B, and selected by almost every customer for the 3A. (Today AiResearch is part of AlliedSignal.)

The electrical system was completely redesigned to improve power distribution, increase reliability and simplify pilot management. The new system was duplicated throughout so that no single fault could lead to complete electrical failure, yet this was done whilst actually reducing the total number of components.

Many of the Series 1B aircraft for non-US markets had had interiors designed by Charles Butler Associates of New York, a firm with long experience in the layout and detail furnishing of airline and executive aircraft. With the Series 3 Charles Butler was not only made the usual consultant on the 'B' aircraft, but also developed a range of improved interiors. These featured a new toilet arrangement, improved galley, new passenger seats and a range of superior furnishing styles and materials. As before, six individual seats remained the most common customer choice, but some required seating for up to ten, often using settees along the sides or across the rear of the cabin.

The first aircraft to this standard was 25111, the 111th HS 125, flown in August 1966 as G-ATYH and ferried as a Series 3A to the United States the following month, there to become N1041B. By this time output of the 125 was steady at seven per month, and just over 50 had been flown out as green aircraft to the three North American distributors. To say Hawker Siddeley was gratified at its penetration of the tough transatlantic market is to put it mildly, but it was evident by 1966 that, as in other markets, many of the customers did not wish to be identified. The reasons were, and to this day continue to be, highly varied. One of the most common reasons for shyness is fear that a company's stockholders might consider an executive jet an expensive luxury, rather than a vital business tool.

In the 1980s British Aerospace, into which Hawker Siddeley was merged in 1977, carried out a confidential survey of all the original customers for the 125. The number of aircraft that could in the slightest degree be considered as "perks" could easily be counted on the fingers of one hand. More than 98 per cent were, and still are, hardworking business tools, purchased for their time-saving (which means money-saving), convenience and security. This is elaborated upon in the final chapter.

Two of the first Series 3B aircraft were purchased by Qantas, at that time called Qantas Empire Airways, for crew training and conversion. The Australian flag carrier had been one of the first potential customers to discuss the 125, and it played a role in the type's development and equipment standard. Whilst appreciating the value of an executive jet to the airline's management, the two aircraft were actually purchased for the specific task of training and qualifying airline pilots. Though simulators were already playing a major role in this task, there has never been any substitute for actual hands-on experience on the real thing, but this is very expensive. Quoting actual costs is rather like "how long is a piece of string", but in 1966 the US Civil Aeronautics Board (CAB) quoted direct operating costs per flight hour on aircraft such as the 707 or DC-8 as being in the range £133 – £246 and depreciation at £43 – £75 per flight hour. Corresponding costs for the 125 worked out at £35 and £15, assuming a utilisation of 2,000 hours per year. Moreover, using a "big jet" for crew training means a loss of revenue and possibly disruption of schedules

A Series 3B/RA, operated by Daimler-Benz A.G. Note the ventral fin which distinguished /RA aircraft.

The first Qantas aircraft, VH-ECE, was the first 125 to be fitted with the Mk.522 engine, and its delivery was delayed by the loss of a turbine blade as previously mentioned. Once it reached Sydney this aircraft worked harder, in terms of number of takeoffs and landings, than any other 125, eventually logging 53,882 landings in 15 years. Popularly called The Pocket Rocket, it bore the total load, from 1970 onwards, of carrying out the two hours of practice flying in command and licence renewal of over 200 second officers on 707s and 747s. Its cockpit was as far as possible styled and arranged to resemble the 707-138B. The need for airlines to do their pilot training has ebbed and flowed over the years, but thousands of co-pilots, called variously First Officers or Second Officers, would give their right arms for a 125 in which they could quickly gain command experience.

Well before the Series 3 became available, the Hatfield designers had finalised their plans for increasing the aircraft's range. There was no prospect yet of any new engine or a new wing, but at affordable cost it was possible to effect a modest increase in fuel capacity. But, more than this, the detailed study of the 125 had shown that further small changes could reduce aerodynamic drag.

The upgraded aircraft were designated Series 3A/RA and 3B/RA, the RA standing for Range Added. The most significant change was the greater fuel capacity, and this was developed as a customer option on the Series 3 and even flown on one Series 1B, aircraft 25094. Lacking room in the wing, the extra capacity was provided by adding a completely new tank under the rear fuselage. This has a capacity of 112 Imperial gallons (509 litres), and is attached beneath the pressurised fuselage by three bolts.

Side fairings are added to give a smooth streamlined exterior, and, as many expected, addition of the tank made a major contribution to the reduction in drag. At the rear of the tank a tapered fairing and a tail bumper was added.

Addition of the extended-range tank required relocation of the fuel filter, filter deicing tank and pumps forward of the wing. It also required the design of a new flap operating mechanism. This replaced the hydraulic ram with a hydraulic motor giving a rotary output. The strong skid along the centreline of the belly was retained, but the flap hinge at its rear end was eliminated, making a useful contribution to the drag reduction. There was no change to the ram-operated airbrakes, interconnected with the new flap motor to provide the lift-dump facility with the flaps at 50 degrees.

Typical of the original de Havilland wish to keep everything simple had been the omission of fairing doors over the retracted main wheels.

The Brazilian Air Force has been a long term operator of a number of 125 variants with a pair of its early Series 3B/RCs seen here flying in formation.

This was the first Series 3B/RA and was operated for many years by the Civil Aviation Flying Unit.

Careful tunnel testing showed that addition of such doors would be well worthwhile, and they were accordingly made standard on the 3/RA series aircraft.

Altogether, the improved rear-fuselage shape, elimination of the central flap hinge and addition of mainwheel doors reduced drag by about five per cent. This resulted in a 10 knot increase in maximum cruising speed, but was more often used to reduce fuel consumption. Overall, quite minor modifications enabled the 3/RA aircraft to carry full payload for about 1,500 nautical miles.

The tail bumper, the fairing for which gave it a secondary duty as a ventral fin, was necessary to protect the extended-range fuel tank in the unlikely event of a wheels-up landing.

Another significant change was to redesign the so-called DA panel, the main electrical power distribution panel behind the co-pilot's seat. Instead of having fuses on its rear face, circuit-breakers were fitted, and

these were mounted on the front and side faces where they are visible to the crew. This change also enabled each wiring loom to be manufactured on the bench instead of by individual circuit assembly inside the aircraft.

G-AVRG, a Series 3B/RA, was used to carry out a gruelling tour of Latin America covering 40,000 miles in 46 days, plus 95 separate demonstration flights in 15 countries. It involved using some of the world's highest airfields, operating in ambient temperatures from -30°C to +40°C, and in such humidity that one of the crew claimed to be using more silica gel than kerosene! In Paraguay it seemed that most of all three fighting services turned up at Asuncion Airport, with President Stroessner, presumably trying to introduce some excitement into the proceedings, asking, "Can you do a low beat-up?"

Here, after working in 43°C in the shade all day, one of the crew was reduced to shouting the most foul English oaths he could conjure up in order to keep visitors off the aircraft. Undaunted by the language, one of the visitors quietly asked, "I'm the British Ambassador, would you permit me to bring my wife and daughter on board?"

Perhaps the shortest story of this big trip concerns the pilot who came back into the cabin, on a landing approach, somewhere in the Andes, and said to the distinguished passengers, "Would you mind if I admire the view for a moment?" He didn't like to say that the undercarriage indicator on the flight deck wasn't working, and he wanted to see if the pin indicator was sticking up through the wing!

One of the major customers for early 125s was the FAB (Brazilian Air Force) which bought five Series 3B/RCs, to which were later added more. (The /RC variant differed from the /RA in that it had a ramp weight and maximum takeoff weight increased by 300 lb and a zero fuel weight increased by 500 lb.)

The FAB currently has twelve of Series 3, 400 and 700. The Grupo Transport Especial use sits jets for VIP transport based at Brasilia, and for flight inspection and calibration duties based at Rio de Janeiro. One aircraft is also used for radar and equipment evaluation. This is one of the world's biggest fleets of 125s, and all the FAB aircraft are used intensively, the squadron logging 100,000 hours by 1985. In 1993 they celebrated 25 years of 125 operations at an impressive ceremony in Brasilia where a granite monument to the aircraft was unveiled.

Having braved the worst that Latin America could do, G-AVRG then carried out one of the toughest sales trips on record. Lasting 87 days, it involved flying 105,000 miles in 270 hours throughout the Far East. On 44 takeoffs the tyre pressure had to be set at only 75 lb/sq in, and at the tiny strip at Anduki, Brunei, the surface was a grassy sand which contrived to be critical from the viewpoint of moisture content. When wet it was extremely slippery and pliable, with poor bearing qualities; when dry it was soft sand, resulting in problems with acceleration on takeoff. In either condition the strip also provided "punishing bumps". Romeo Golf took everything in its stride, incidentally repeatedly demonstrating that an APU in some parts of the world is essential.

An early 125 charter operator was Midwestern Airlines, based at Detroit. Its first 125 had "covered the Americas from the Yukon to the Caribbean" when it was called upon to make a 30,000-mile round trip to Proserpine, Queensland, Australia. On return to Detroit, Midwestern President George L. Kittle checked through customs, announcing that he had come that day from London. The customs official, looking at the small jet, said ,"You don't need customs clearance on a flight from Canada". Kittle replied ,"I don't mean London, Ontario, we've come from the other London".

The changes introduced in the extended-range 3/RA aircraft were extremely cost-effective. Hawker Siddeley offered them as a customer retrofit, though of course this had to be carried out by an approved organisation such as a 125 distributor. The first 3/RA aircraft was G-ATHH, which was actually a Series 1B, No 25094. In 1979 this aircraft was sold to Saudi Arabia as HZ-BOI, having been operated in Britain by Granada TV and GKN. Several other Series 1 and 3 aircraft were given some or all of the extended-range modifications, but the whole exercise kept the pressure on the designers to keep on improving the basic 125. ✈

6
The Series 400

By April 1968 total sales of the Hawker amounted to 142. Of these, 116 were for export, 85 of them to North America. Sales were holding up quite well – indeed no fewer than 50 aircraft were to be sold in that calendar year – but Hawker Siddeley was only too keenly aware that it dare not rest on these considerable laurels. The competition was getting sharper every week. New business jets were coming into production, and the existing rivals were being improved. Worldwide experience of executive and related jet operations was, by 1968, approaching one million hours, of which over 100,000 had been logged by the 125 family. And many customers who had bought early aircraft were now looking for improved replacements or additional aircraft. Hawker Siddeley had to respond to the continuing challenge.

Though the funding required for each successive new development might, by today's standards, seem modest, it was often very difficult to persuade the board that the new version was necessary. The task of persuasion fell primarily upon the Hatfield Managing Director. Following the retirement of Rod Banks, this post was held for many years (1965-78) by Jim Thorne, who never hesitated in his support for the 125. On being appointed Hatfield-Chester Divisional Chairman, Thorne was succeeded as Managing Director by Mike Goldsmith, who was also a tower of strength to the small 125 team.

In 1968 what was possible was severely limited. Not very much could be done in the way of major modifications. Rolls-Royce could not then

The first 125-400A was 25173 seen at Hatfield before delivery as G-AWMX.

offer any further improvement in the Viper 522 engine (though its Bristol Engine Division began a study programme for a totally new successor, the RB.401). As a result, the next stage in development combined one of two quite significant improvements with several minor changes which, however, made a big difference in payload/range performance and to the task of the pilot.

One thing that had long been desirable was to clean up the external appearance. No less an authority than Chester's Chief Engineer, Rex Griffiths, described the 125 as "something of an ugly duckling alongside the competition". From the start, the British aircraft had sold on its reputation of low costs, toughness and reliability, but the glamorous "bizjet market" was increasingly becoming influenced by appearance. Accordingly, what had begun as the Series 4, and by early 1968 had been designated the 400 to assist marketing (especially in North America), was a major effort at making the aircraft look better without actually altering the airframe significantly. One obvious change was to get rid of external radio antennas. Previous 125s had prominent external

antennas for ADF sense and HF communications. A few, such as the intensively-used aircraft of Bowater Paper, were equipped with multiple HF wire antennas linking the cockpit, rear fuselage and fin. Nearly all had either one or two parallel rigid "towel rail" ADF sense antennas along the top of the rear fuselage. It was the latter that were thought to need replacement. Wire antennas continued to be a customer option, but the rails were eliminated in the Series 400, being replaced by a suppressed notch antenna in the leading edge of the dorsal fin, as had first appeared on the RAF's Dominies.

Drag was reduced by extending the wing/fuselage fairing forwards. This fairing had always been rather bluff, except in the case of the RAF's Dominies which had the doppler antenna. The reduction in drag produced by adding the rear-fuselage tank and improving the aft end of the wing/fuselage fairing on the Series 3/RA aircraft prompted the design team to tunnel-test improvements at the front. Very quickly a shape was achieved which looked good and achieved an optimum reduction in drag. The resulting fairing weighed almost the same as the bluff shape but extended forwards as far as the entrance door. Further work was aimed at improving the overall smoothness of the fuselage exterior. All these changes were relatively simple to introduce to production, and achieved the dual aims of reducing drag and improving appearance.

Probably the biggest single change in the Series 400 concerned the entrance door. In 1960 de Havilland was still not convinced of the integrity of outward-opening doors in pressurised fuselages. By 1968 thousands of such doors were in use around the world, and there was no longer any justification in adhering to the plug-type upward-sliding pattern. In its place came a totally new outward-opening door, hinged at the bottom, which accomplished three things simultaneously. As had been done in other aircraft, it was simplicity itself to make such a door serve as the integral stairway, merely by building four suitable steps into it. This change alone greatly increased convenience and reduced weight and cost. By not having to be stowed behind the baggage the new door added about 40 per cent to the depth of shelving available for baggage. Not least, the width of the door was reduced from 36 inches to 27. This was still abundantly wide enough for the most difficult passenger or carry-on baggage, but the extra 9 inches of cabin length proved most useful. Charles Butler Associates and other interior designers were able to come up with a range of new internal arrangements. The only major structural change in the vestibule area was that the avionics racking was made vertical instead of horizontal.

A further important improvement in the Series 400 was redesign of the cabin soundproofing. Whilst leaving the thickness of the interior trim unchanged, this brought about a further improvement in the already satisfactory noise-level from the cockpit to the rear pressure bulkhead. One is reminded that on one of the very first test flights in 1962 the passengers included R.E. Bishop, the most eminent of all de Havilland designers. He landed in a state of agitation saying, "There's no point in going on. Nobody will buy it. The noise-level is appalling", apparently forgetting that the prototype was totally devoid of soundproofing or, indeed, any internal furnishing. It makes quite a difference!

The Series 400 was announced at the 1968 Farnborough Air Show, and shown for the first time at the US NBAA (National Business Aircraft

Association) show at Houston, Texas, in October 1968. By this time the decision had been taken to increase maximum takeoff weight (MTOW) by 500 lb to 23,300 lb, and then again to 23,800 lb, the designation becoming Series 403. This was yet a further plus. With each new version up to the Series 800 it has proved possible to increase zero fuel weight to carry more payload and then also increase MTOW to maintain full range. With each change, a knot or two had to be knocked off V_{mo} (maximum operating speed).

There were also refinements to the Series 400 cockpit, many of them the result of suggestions from pilots during the first 175,000 hours of 125 operation. They included a more comfortable pilot seat, individual ventilation for each pilot, and redesign of the cockpit side consoles to increase elbow room. The main instrument panel was reshaped and revised in many details, and the central pedestal was also improved. A particular detail was the introduction of flashing warnings in the handles of the engine HP cocks and fire extinguisher controls, triggered by certain major warning indications.

The first 125-400 featured a full set of undercarriage doors, cleaning up the underside. Also seen here is the rear fuselage fuel tank.

Not least, by late 1968 the Mk.522 engine had had its TBO doubled to 1,600 hours, equivalent to about 600,000 miles. In contrast to what happened to the very first Mk.522 aircraft, the engine had become the most reliable fitted to any executive jet, and this was considered by Hawker Siddeley to be a powerful reason for sticking to it.

It was a matter of the utmost importance to Hawker Siddeley that the Series 400 should be well received. It emerged just as competition was becoming really intense, especially in the North American market, and there was a twinge of fear that distributors and potential customers might think some of the modifications a mere cosmetic facelift, not addressing the deeper issues. What actually happened was that emergence of the Series 400 came at a time of record sales, 50 aircraft being sold in 1968 and another 44 in 1969. The first 125-400A was c/n 25173, delivered across the Atlantic in September 1968. Production continued until July 1973, when number 25290 was delivered as one of six for the FAB (Brazilian Air Force), five for communications and the sixth

specially equipped for checking and calibrating ground electronic navigation and landing aids. The total run of the 125-400 amounted to an excellent 117 aircraft.

One of the early customers for the Series 400 was the South African Air Force, which bought a fleet of specially equipped aircraft which they named *Mercurius*, the Afrikaans rendering of the Roman "messenger of the Gods". Among many other things they were equipped to launch underwing rockets, though their primary mission was VIP transport. Sensitive about the sale, even 20 years ago, Hawker Siddeley identified the customer only as "Stock Scheme C" (other 125s being As or Bs). They have performed predictably well, except for one absolutely unbelievable occasion when, in good visibility, three *Mercurius* flew in formation into Table Mountain...

Another country had a 125-400B which played a part in a shooting war. The Argentine Fenix Escuadron was hastily formed in April 1982 to fly various kinds of communications and support missions during

The integral airstairs door, introduced on the Series 400, is shown on this aircraft for the South African Air Force, locally know as Mercurius. *The SAAF has operated 125s for over 25 years.*

The Argentine Navy used its 125-400 very effectively, if unusually, during the Falklands campaign.

the war with Britain over the Falkland Islands (known by the Argentinians as the Malvinas). The 125, aircraft 25251, which had previously been in service with the Argentinian Armada (navy), made many sorties. Tasks included acting as navigation lead ship to Daggers and Skyhawks, and acting as a decoy by making feint attacks to draw off the Royal Navy's feared Sea Harriers, a particularly dangerous operation which called for the 125 to fly towards the battle-zone at altitude and, just before interception, to dive steeply and fly back to base at very low level over the sea. It also acted as an airborne radio relay station between the command centre at Port Stanley and low-flying Argentine attack aircraft, giving the latter real-time information on target areas and, in particular, where the Sea Harriers were. Several people in British Aerospace continued to receive Christmas cards from Buenos Aires, even in 1982, and friendships have been restored.

By the time the Series 400 was in production, Hatfield/Chester had matured – some would say they had been educated by the customers – and knew how to offer excellent interiors and, at least as important, how to price them. The problem had hardly arisen with the simpler interior of the Dove, but with the 125 it was often tough going. According to Jack Garston, who was General Manager at Chester, "If the customer sent the chief pilot all we had to do was talk avionics and we could agree on the exact build-standard within hours. If they sent the President's wife we might be in for days of discussion on layouts, fabrics, colours and special furnishing ideas. Let's face it – some of the early aircraft were absolute disasters! However we were soon doing really good interiors, sometimes to a scheme by an outside furnishing design house, although such things were anathema to dyed-in-the-wool production people. They liked standardisation, and the only price they knew for special interiors was *high*! Today there is no problem at all."

Series 400s were soon to be found in use all over the world, in most

Jim Thorne, Managing Director at Hatfield for many years and later Divisional Chairman, is seen here (right) with Les Tuck, who was originally part of the Hatfield-based 125 sales team before moving to the US to become President of Hawker Siddeley Aviation, Inc., in Washington DC.

cases in conventional operations. But things can be different in some parts of Africa. One passenger went to the toilet, only to find it already occupied by a goat. Mentioning this, he was told, "But of course; where else would you put a goat?" Another African country was visited by a Hawker Siddeley team to discuss support for a forthcoming 125 delivery. As the hotel was full up, they were accommodated on an offshore island, thickly populated by giant lizards, spiders and many other off-putting inhabitants. Each morning, clad in their smart city suits, the team would climb into a trailer pulled by a farm tractor – often accompanied by a few dozen boisterous kids – and chug to the airport to discuss the multi-million dollar contract.

Whereas in Africa city suits soon became darkened as perspiration soaked through, it was a bit different on the North Slope of Alaska. In 1975, here at "the top of the world", 850 men were building the trans-Alaska pipeline to the oil terminal at Prudhoe Bay. They had the luxury of a 6,300-foot gravel strip, and a new hangar with doors which were kept shut whenever possible, as opening them cost a minimum of $200 in heat loss and recovery time. Based there, but usually shuttling through the various camp strips along the pipeline route (varying from 5,200 feet to 2,500 feet in length), were three 125s, one belonging to ARCO (Atlantic-Richfield Co) and two to ERA Helicopters

The three jets were kept flying by the strict adoption of special measures, notably concerning tyres (inflated not with air but with absolutely dry nitrogen), batteries (carefully serviced, and deep-cycled every 30 days) and engine oil (kept above -26°C). Pilots learned quickly. "If you taxi through a snow bank with hot brakes they will soon be frozen solid. If everybody turns out to watch your landing, don't land!" A single jet landing or takeoff could generate enough ice fog to shut the airport for an hour or two, but the "de Havillands" never faltered. The ERA maintenance chief in far-away Anchorage said at the time, "Preventative maintenance is the key. We've had one aircraft for four years, logging 2,600 hours, and we've never had to cancel a single flight".

Certainly the 125-400 fully upheld the type's reputation for rugged reliability. Cutler-Hammer, who among other things makes incredibly complex avionics systems for military aircraft, took delivery of a "de Havilland 400A" in December 1969. Eight years later it had logged 4,000 hours, with utilisation rapidly increasing with more trips from Milwaukee to the West Coast and a new plant opening in Sarasota, Florida. So, in 1978, C-H took on board a new Series 700, which like its older partner was full of clever navigation aids – and passenger information cards printed in seven languages including Russian and Japanese! Throughout this time the pilots had been Lee Snow and co-captain Arlyn Clementz. Snow, a 17,000-hour captain, said, "the 125 is more reliable than my car!"

J.C. Bamford, makers of the earthmoving equipment known universally as "JCBs", was an early operator of a Dove. In 1970 Joe Bamford added a 125-400, saying, "in 90 minutes I can get to probably

Halfway there...

The 200th aircraft, a Series 400A, was in final assembly *(picture, below)* on the Chester line in July 1969. On the left is Leonard Shallcross, the senior superintendent responsible for the HS 125 production line. The aircraft, registered N702S and the first of three destined for the retail organisation Sears Roebuck, was rolled out

in September and ferried to Little Rock Airmotive, Arkansas, in early October by Desmond Penrose and John Fricker. The Sears Roebuck order also marked the 100th 125 sales in the USA.

Just over nine years after the 125's maiden flight, the 250th sale of the 125 was celebrated at Hatfield on 15 September 1971 with nine customer aircraft lined up facing four company aircraft *(above)*. Twenty-two flags were flown representing all the countries into which the 125 had been sold. Dennis O'Connor of Texas is recorded as having bought the 250th aircraft, it being the 203rd export 125. The 125 was well on the way to reaching the 500 "target" noted in chapter 1.

The RAF, already a major operator of the 125 with its fleet of Dominies, selected the Series 400B for VIP duties.

something like 90 per cent of all the purchasing power in Europe". Utilising corporate colours, the aircraft was painted in a bright all-yellow scheme with a thick red cheatline along the centre of the fuselage. Inevitably in certain quarters it became irreverently known as "the bleeding banana". In July 1973 the company took delivery of a 125-600, which instead of being all-yellow had a white-top fuselage. Joe (Mr Bamford Senior) was renowned for lying on a car inspection trolley and meticulously examining the underside of each new 125 before accepting it! The company has gone on to acquire progressively a 700, 800 and

1000, and propound a highly positive approach to business aircraft. To quote J.C. Bamford, "If you are in business, invest heavily in aircraft ..... it's not what they cost, it's what they get you".

In December 1969, in an apparent precursor of events that would occur almost exactly 25 years later, it was announced that Hawker Siddeley was joining forces with Beech Aircraft Corporation, of Wichita,

Kansas. The famed US general-aviation manufacturer, which had for years been studying the executive jet market and had even experimented with putting jet engines on a King Air, at last decided not to produce an aircraft of its own but to sew up a major deal for an established type.

In fact informal contact had been made with Beech many years earlier. In 1961 Frank Lloyd, Hatfield Sales Manager, met in Paris with Beech's Vice-President of Sales to talk about the proposed 125 programme. Beech acknowledged that it "needed to get into the act". The 125 appeared right for the US market and it would be wasteful for Beech to duplicate all of the design, development and tooling costs to come up with its own, similar, aeroplane. However it felt that it was essential that the aircraft have an American engine, American instruments and avionics if it was to succeed in the States. Lloyd suggested that Hatfield could sell Beech bare airframes for completion in America. Although the proposal progressed no further at the time it laid the seeds for what was to happen eight years later.

Under the terms of the 1969 deal, Beech replaced Atlantic Aviation, Atlantic Aviation of Canada (previously Timmins) and AiResearch as distributors for all 125s in North America. In this market it was agreed the aircraft would be renamed the Beechcraft Hawker BH-125. Beech agreed to purchase 40 green aircraft from Hawker Siddeley and complete them as BH-125s to customer requirements.

Under a further part of the agreement the two companies agreed to collaborate on the design of two new business jets. One, the BH-600, would be a larger and faster version of the 125. The other, the BH-200, would be an entirely new and smaller aircraft, notable for its short-field performance, which had begun life as the projected D.H.135.

To claim that the deal with Beech Aircraft made the existing distributors of the 125 in North America bitter would be an understatement, but they could see its attraction for Hawker Siddeley. An immediate order for 40 aircraft was surely good business, and Beech claimed that with its gigantic network of dealers it could turn in a superior performance in finding and signing up customers. In fact it did not turn out that way. The buoyant sales of 1968-69 gradually turned into a severe slump, which hit the United States harder than most countries.

Even the initial kick-off batch of 40 aircraft could not all be sold. Moreover, the work on the new BH-600 brought to light differences in philosophy and design practice which made it difficult to continue as a joint operation, and the BH-200 never progressed beyond the initial brochure and a wooden mockup in Hatfield's Experimental Hangar.

J.C. Bamford's striking colour scheme of bright all-yellow with a thick red cheatline along the centre of the fuselage used on its Series 400B. Slightly less yellow was used on the company's later 125s.

During the original agreement with Beech Aircraft, the version sold in the States was known as the BH 125. N3711L, one such designated aircraft, was a visitor to Hatfield in July 1969.

Eventually the partnership was amicably severed in September 1975. Little did anyone dream at the time that Beech and the 125 would finally wed 19 years later. At the NBAA show at New Orleans a month later. Hawker Siddeley announced that a new North American marketing organisation had been established. Hawker Siddeley Aviation Inc, previously set up for the abortive first launch of the HS 146, was resurrected to handle HS 125 sales in the USA and Mexico. It took over previously padlocked premises at Washington DC, with Les Tuck as President. To cover Canada, Innotech Aviation was appointed; this was in effect the original Canadian distributor, Timmins, under a new name. To support customers, servicing was returned to the two original distributors, Atlantic Aviation (which had added a base at Houston, Texas, to its headquarters at Wilmington), and AiResearch Aviation (which likewise had added to its facility at Los Angeles bases at Houston and Long Island). To look after the North and Midwest a third approved service centre was appointed, K-C Aviation (Kimberley Clark, best known for its "Kleenex" products) of Appleton, Wisconsin. Subsequently this network of service centres was to be expanded and otherwise altered, as explained later.

7

The Series 600

When Hawker Siddeley arrived at an agreement with Beech Aircraft, the 125-600 was already the subject of detailed engineering design at Hatfield. Though at one time influenced by the collaborative agreement, this influence quickly waned, and the eventual aircraft was entirely the responsibility of Hawker Siddeley. It was made possible solely because Rolls-Royce had developed a new family of Viper turbojets, the Mk.600 series, offering a further increase in power.

Adopting this engine, and making use of the extra thrust, were far from being clear-cut choices. By the late 1960s the turbojet was obsolescent if not obsolete as far as commercial jetliners were concerned. Its place was fast being taken by what Rolls-Royce had called the bypass jet and the Americans had more slickly named the turbofan. Non-technical people also called such engines fanjets, and the word meant a substantial reduction in fuel burn and a dramatic reduction in noise. During the 1960s many communities were becoming far more noise conscious than they had been in the early days of jets, partly because of increased traffic, and such powerful certification authorities as the FAA and British ARB (now the CAA) were drawing up legislation which promised to prohibit the production of aircraft that were unable to meet numerically specified noise standards. Unfortunately, the Mk.600 Viper promised to be even noisier than the 500-series, as well as heavier, but it offered a modest increase in thrust and a modest reduction in specific fuel consumption, gained mainly by the use of a two-stage turbine. The Viper 600 prototype first ran in August 1966, and from July 1969 its development was undertaken in collaboration with Fiat of Italy. It was announced that the civil Mk.601 version would have a takeoff rating of 3,750 lb.

It would have been possible merely to substitute these engines for the Mk.522 in the 125-400, and such an aircraft was studied as the Series 500. It would have minimised the development cost and risk, but would not have done a lot for the aircraft beyond giving it startling takeoff and climb performance. This would have been of interest to those few operators who frequented hot-and-high airfields, but most customers would have been disappointed. Raising the thrust from 3,360 to 3,750 lb would be enough for the 125 to be increased substantially in weight. Without major redesign it would not have been simple to find

G-ARYC, the first production 125, was used by Rolls-Royce to flight test the Viper 601 engine that was to power the 125-600.

room for much more fuel, but an alternative way of using the available increase in weight was to stretch the fuselage. All 125s had been the same length after the first two prototypes, and though almost all existing customers were very satisfied with the aircraft, it was obvious that lengthening the cabin would considerably increase the versatility and appeal of all future 125s. As had been the case for a long time, not a lot could yet be done about the incessant need for greater range.

As finally agreed, the improvements introduced in the 125-600 were the most extensive on any version up to that time. The new model could be identified at a glance by the longer fuselage, with an extra window, and a taller and thus more pointed fin. But there was much more to it than this, with changes extending to the fuel system and weights, the more powerful engines, ailerons, elevators, electrics, avionics and a wide range of furnishings.

The fuselage was lengthened by 24 inches by the insertion of a new bay in line with the front of the wing/fuselage fairing. This bay incorporated a window on each side, restoring the six-a-side configuration seen on early Series 1s. Another change to the fuselage was to remove the glassfibre fairing above the cockpit and reprofile the actual pressurised fuselage to give minimum drag and an improved appearance.

Towards the same ends several further changes were made. The radome was extended forwards by 6 inches and thus made more pointed. The dorsal fin was extended forwards almost as far as the last passenger window (this was connected with adding fuel capacity, as explained later). The ventral fin was extended forwards to give a horizontal bottom line. The entire tail group was strengthened to handle the increased weights and higher manoeuvre speeds, and the overfin (the portion of fin above the horizontal tail) was increased in height by 9 inches to maintain directional stability.

Redesign of the wing, and many other features of the Series 600, were the responsibility of Max Roberts, who had rejoined the programme. The wing was unchanged aerodynamically, but the structure was redesigned to accept the increased loads caused by the greater weights and higher speeds. Among the major differences were that the front spar, previously fabricated, was integrally machined; the centre

The first 125-600 was aircraft 25256, G-AYBH, a Series 400 converted on the production line at Chester.

spar was strengthened; the upper and lower skins, previously stepped, were machined to give continuous root-to-tip taper; a baffle was added forming an inner skin beneath the upper surface to contain fuel in the event of an abnormally heavy landing fracturing a main-leg trunnion and rupturing the upper skin; and stringers, ribs and skins were generally thickened.

Several changes were made to the flight control system. To improve handling, the aileron gear ratio was lowered, gearing was added to the trim tab on the left aileron, and the right aileron was fitted with two geared tabs instead of one. Fairings were added over the elevator hinges and it was found that these considerably improved elevator operation throughout flight. The flaps were unchanged although the maximum angle was reduced from 50 to 45 degrees.

Of course, the main landing gears had to be strengthened. Wheel and tyre sizes remained unchanged, but the brakes were increased in capacity and controlled by a later type of Dunlop Maxaret anti-skid system. The only change necessary on the nose gear was strengthening of the towing lug.

Apart from having a two-stage turbine, the Viper Mk.601 introduced several other differences. The most important were a new short annular combustion chamber and an increase in mass flow of about ten per cent. The increase in engine dry weight was quite acceptable, from 760 to 790 lb. The new engine picked up on unchanged mountings, but the pylon and cowling were altered. To accommodate the greater airflow the inlet diameter was increased by approximately one inch, but the rest of the pod was if anything made more slender, especially in plan view. This effect was heightened by the fact that the Mk.602 was a longer engine, and fitted with a longer jetpipe, so the result was an improvement

Long term 125 operator, J.C. Bamford, regularly traded up to the latest model. This photo shows its newly acquired 600B with noise-suppression nozzles, (foreground), flying with the company's about-to-be-disposed-of unsuppressed Series 600B.

in appearance which paralleled that gained from the longer fuselage. The circular rear fairing was specially designed to carry a silencer.

Though both the engine and aircraft manufacturers had studied the problem of noise from the earliest days of the 125, the pressure to do something about it was at first minimal. Despite the deafening environment experienced by Mr Bishop riding in the bare metal fuselage of the prototype, there had never been a problem about internal cabin noise in the completed aircraft, albeit that the standard was achieved with a considerable weight penalty. External noise was another matter, and, following a hardening of public attitudes in developed countries, noise legislation was drawn up by several certification authorities. The leaders were the United States, where FAR (Federal Air Regulations) Part 36 was published, with a compliance date of 1 July 1974, and the United Kingdom, where UK/ICAO Annex 16 was adopted with a compliance date of 1 January 1976.

These compliance dates applied to all new aircraft. Though the timing was slightly relaxed for existing aircraft, it was evident that they, too, would progressively have to meet the new noise requirements or be withdrawn from use. In the longer term, the requirements were to become progressively more severe, strongly accelerating the shift from turbojets to the much quieter turbofans, but when the 125 Series 600 was introduced in 1972 the obvious thing to do was to develop a silencer – perhaps more correctly called a noise-suppressing nozzle – which would enable this aircraft to meet the legislation in 1974/76. More than 20 years earlier Rolls-Royce, notably in the person of F.B. Greatrex, Chief Installation Engineer, had begun development of robust and simple nozzles which greatly reduced noise by increasing the length of the periphery to promote more rapid mixing of the jet efflux with the atmosphere. In 1973 a nozzle of this type was first fitted to an HS 125. It was very similar to those fitted to the Comet 4 family, breaking the jet into eight lobes. Various other nozzles were also tested, as was the effect of acoustic blankets around the jetpipe. It was soon established that the requirement could be met by the compliance date, and that suitable "hushkits" could be made available for retrofit on Series 600 aircraft then in service.

The Hatfield designers studied several possible ways of increasing fuel capacity, and for the Series 600 they decided to add a 50-gallon tank in the dorsal fin above the rear fuselage. This occupied the location

Alpa S.A. of Spain acquired a Series 600B configured in a convertible ambulance layout.

of the ADF sense antennas, which explained the forwards extension of the dorsal fin, the ram-air inlet moving to a location about 4 feet ahead of the rear pressure bulkhead. The new tank was a simple light-alloy box which formed the actual skin of the aircraft, though it was completely unstressed and readily removable. Raising total fuel capacity to 1,187 Imperial gallons was accompanied by clearance of the Series 600 to an MTOW of 25,000 lb, with corresponding significant increases in MLW and ZFW. This enabled full payload of six passengers and baggage to be flown, with full reserves, for 1,570 nautical miles, which was a significant advance and made one-stop US coast-to-coast operation child's play. At the same time, pressure remained for such flights to be possible without an intermediate stop . This could already be achieved by the Gulfstream II, a much larger and more expensive aircraft than the 125, but in France, Dassault was building the prototype of the long-range

An early advertising shot of the Series 600. The cars really were parked around the aircraft, but the building in the background was put in as separate artwork afterwards.

Falcon 50. Clearly, it was only a matter of time before coast-to-coast range would be expected of smaller business jets.

Whilst developing the Series 600, the Hatfield and Chester teams collaborated with Beech Aircraft to define many further upgrades and improvements. Some of the most extensive were to be found in the cockpit. The CWS (central warning system) was redesigned as a Master Warning System with annunciators on the roof and centre panels. The instrument panels, glare shield, side consoles, central pedestal, avionics panel, control knobs and bulkhead trim were all restyled – which didn't leave much unchanged.

Systems changes centred on the electrics and avionics, but also included fitting thermostatic cabin temperature control, simplified engine starting and simplified engine anti-icing. A completely new addition was a pressure reoiling system supplied by a 2.5-gallon auxiliary tank in the rear equipment bay and which gave a total of 17 hours' flying before the need to refill the system.

Though similar, the electrical system was modified in numerous details including the addition of a Flitetronic solid-state standby inverter, rated at 250 VA, handling all essential AC supplies.

Collins remained the standard supplier of avionics, while RCA supplied the weather radar, ATC transponder and DME. The more pointed radome had no effect on radar performance. The Series 600 retained the option of HF, the usual fit being a Sunair system. The number two VHF antenna was relocated at the aft end of the underwing centreline skid and the ADF loops moved rearwards. Addition of the dorsal tank required the ADF sense antennas to be moved into an extended dorsal fin.

Options on the 600 included doppler, Decca Navigator, flight-data recorder, passenger-address system and equipment for operation in low weather minima (ICAO Category II). A "feature console" was provided in the cabin for fitting such items as a time clock, digital readouts and a telephone.

While the numerous possible refinements in interior design were being worked out in detail, partly in collaboration with Charles Butler and other interior design consultants, two Series 400 aircraft on the line at Chester were taken aside for completion as the prototypes of the Series

600. Many of the systems and other details of these aircraft had already been incorporated to Series 400 standard, so they were eventually to appear more or less as Series 400s with the Mk.601 engines and the visible airframe alterations. The first, airframe, number 25256, was registered as G-AYBH and flew on 21 January 1971. The second, 25258, was completed only days later, but at this point a major hiccup occurred in the supply of engines. For reasons connected solely with the company's large new RB.211 turbofan engine, mighty Rolls-Royce was driven to bankruptcy. The British Government promptly nationalised the assets, forming Rolls-Royce (1971) Ltd, but as all previous contracts were void, no business could be done, and no Vipers could be supplied to Chester until fresh contracts had been agreed with the new Rolls-Royce company. Eventually 25258 was completed as G-AZHS and flown on 25 November 1971.

The two Series 600B development aircraft were certainly by far the best-looking 125s to date, and their flight development more than confirmed their superior performance and handling. Internally they featured upgraded passenger seats, carpets and fabrics, redesigned roof light and air louvre fittings (the latter now being flush instead of projecting), and with seats, refreshment/galley modules and other items rail-mounted to facilitate changes in configuration.

The Hawker Siddeley board, which had from the very beginning sanctioned each successive batch of committed production aircraft – sometimes, as in 1970-71, slightly in advance of sales – authorised the manufacture of an initial batch of 38 of the new Series 600 aircraft, which in 1971 was considerably more than had been sold. The period was a bleak one, with a general malaise in Western industrial markets, quite apart from the bankruptcy of Rolls-Royce. The first production aircraft, which started a new sequence of constructor's numbers at 26001, was also the first 600A. Initially registered G-AZUF, it was completed in early-1972 and flown out to Wichita in May, where it was completed and furnished as the BH 125-600 demonstrator, registered N82BH. The first customers for the 125-600B were the Green Shield Stamp Trading Company and the Ministry of Defence. The latter procured two aircraft, with military registrations XX507 and XX508 and designated CC Mk.2s, which served as executive transports with No.32

Squadron, Royal Air Force, based at Northolt. Here they joined four Series 400 aircraft, designated as CC Mk.1s. Subsequently No.32 Squadron, which has both RAF and Royal Navy crews and provides VIP transport for the British Government, distinguished visitors, and occasionally members of The Royal Family, was also to receive the 125

A trial installation on 125-600 G-AZHS was a survey camera pod mock-up fitted over the main cabin access door. The aircraft did fly in this condition, with no adverse handling characteristics.

Series 700. (No.32 Squadron has since incorporated The Royal Flight and is now known as No.32 The Royal Squadron.)

Though it was not in production very long, the Series 600 was important to many operators in Europe. They include Transair France (Air Affaires), the charter operator Lyon Air (whose 600B replaced a 3B which in turn had replaced a 1B), the famed champagne house of Moët et Chandon (again this 600B replaced an earlier model, a 3B), and Alpa Air Taxis of Spain. Before it got its 125-600B the Spanish operator leased a Series 400B, and in the first four weeks of operation (in February 1975) flew 68 hours and visited 61 destinations. Four months later the 600B arrived at the Bilbao base, and has since operated intensively as a convertible executive transport/air ambulance. Alpa air Taxis was one of many operators which capitalised on the 125's versatility for use in non-corporate roles.

In 1975 a garishly painted 600B was delivered to the West German BFS at Frankfurt. The Bundesanstalt für Flugsicherung (Federal office for air traffic control) already operated a fleet of Doves and HS (Avro) 748s, but these could not reach the high altitudes to which the airways system had been extended. There was no argument about the choice of jet; except at far greater cost, only the 125 could operate to 45,000 feet, accommodate the operator console and equipment for checking both

For high altitude airways aids calibration the German Bundesanstalt Für Flugsicherung (BFS) operated this specially equipped 125-600. The aircraft could be quickly converted from its flight inspection role to seven-seat VIP transport.

This 600B, operated by the UK Ministry of Defence, was one of two 125s to be heavily modified for the Blue Vixen radar trials programme. Changes included re-configuring the flight deck to represent a Sea Harrier FRS.2, the nose modified to accept the radar installation and, on this aircraft, a launch-rail complete with an AIM-9L Sidewinder acquisition round installed under the starboard wing.

civil and military navigation aids, provide a very stable platform for long periods, and as a secondary role serve as a seven-passenger VIP aircraft for Federal ministers. The Viper 601s were fitted with multilobe noise suppressors.

The BFS aircraft is registered D-CFSK. An even more elaborately equipped aircraft is D-CFCF, owned by Conti-Flug of Cologne and operated by Lufthansa's subsidiary Condor Flugdienst. Between 24 July and 26 August 1974 it carried out a far-reaching, highly-specialised meteorological survey for the Max-Planck Institute for Chemistry at Mainz and the Met Institute of Frankfurt University. The object was to measure the distribution of gases such as hydrogen, carbon monoxide and ozone, and to analyse the content of nitrogen dioxide, methane and mercury, over a continuous north/south profile covering the entire length of the Americas. The survey was expected to provide new understanding about the origins, life cycle and decomposition of the gases. DFVLR, the Federal flight research institute, filled the entire left side of the cabin with sensors, analysers and recorders. The route was down the west coast to Punta Arenas, at the southern tip of South America, and then from Panama up the east coast of North America on the return.

One of the most "special" 125s ever to have flown bears the British military registration ZF130: it is a former Saudi Arabian-owned 125-600B now on British Ministry of Defence charge but bailed (freely loaned) to Ferranti Defence Systems (now part of GEC Avionics). In September 1989 it began a new life as one of the two 125 trials aircraft (the other being the RAE's Series 1, c/n 25009) for integration of the Blue Vixen radar and various weapon systems. Blue Vixen is the advanced multimode radar fitted to the Royal Navy's Sea Harrier FRS.2s (a totally upgraded aircraft), its early flight development having been done with a BAe (BAC) One-Eleven testbed. Unlike the big One-Eleven, the 125 has a completely rebuilt flight deck, the right half of which represents the FRS.2 cockpit. Weapons to be integrated include AIM-9L Sidewinder and AIM-120A AMRAAM (advanced medium range air-to-air missile). The weapon systems are simulated on board, and the missiles (or captive versions, *see photo on previous page*) can be carried on underwing pylons. This aircraft was later used in developing the ECR-90 radar for the European Fighter Aircraft (Eurofighter 2000).

In many respects the Series 600 was an important advance. Its appearance wiped away for ever any suggestion that the 125 was an "ugly duckling", and its interior was so good it changed little for some considerable time afterwards. In flight performance, also, the new model left little to be desired, except in the single matter of range. In long-range cruise the Series 600 offered only about another 60 to 70 nautical miles, and some customers wanted a lot more than this. Despite these improvements, all was not well with 125 marketing.

Problems with the engine supplier were gradually being resolved, as Rolls-Royce (1971) Ltd got into its stride and once again began delivering to its customers. Problems between Hawker Siddeley and Beech continued, and, as noted earlier, the partnership was eventually discontinued during the period that the Series 600 was in production. The real problem however was the engine; although in many ways an excellent power plant, the need to replace it rapidly became insistent. The problem of range has been mentioned repeatedly. The problem of noise legislation was looming up fast, with US requirements due to come into force only a year after the start of deliveries of the 600A to US customers. Already the 125 was the only medium-size executive jet not fitted with quieter and more efficient turbofan engines. The last straw was what history has called "the oil crisis". In 1973 the Middle East oil producing nations suddenly increased the price of oil dramatically for various political reasons. Within two years aviation fuel prices rose roughly by a factor of ten – say, from 11 cents to $1.20 a gallon – and this was the final blow that forced Hawker Siddeley to switch to a different engine.

Thus, coupled with the overall business recession in the early to mid-1970s, the Series 600 did not achieve the big production it deserved. Only 72 were built, the last being 26071, delivered in November 1976. But the Series 600 was basically an excellent aircraft. For example, Captain Beau Younghusband, Chief Pilot of Rio Tinto Zinc, said in 1975, "It is a fact that many people have the impression of company-owned jets as some sort of infrequently used luxury vehicles, available only for the whimsical use of a select body of executives or individuals.... As far as my company is concerned, our 125 Series 600 is a workhorse. In the first full month of operation, we moved more than 250 people on 40 sectors over a distance of over 30,000 miles. This took 68.5 hours; our average speed overall was 440 mph, and on our 'milk run' trips we averaged 462 mph."

While many 600s are still giving good service, a number of others were re-engined. As described in Chapter 9, the re-engined aircraft are identified by an 'F' prefix, for "fan". The prototype of the next version, the Series 700, was actually the second 600B re-engined, and so to this day it is more accurately called an F600. To the purist it would be a stretched F400. ✈

8
The Series 700

The advantages of a turbofan engine were fully appreciated even before the original D.H.125 was being designed in 1960. Briefly, such an engine has a large LP (low-pressure) compressor, or fan, driven by a separate LP turbine. Air passing through the inner part of the fan goes into the HP (high-pressure) compressor, part of what is called the core engine, the rest of which comprises the combustion chamber and turbines. The rest of the fan delivery is either ejected straight to atmosphere through a peripheral nozzle ring or else bypassed round the core to be mixed with the hot core jet in the final nozzle.

In either event, the net result is that, whilst a turbojet imparts an extremely high velocity to a small-diameter very hot jet, the turbofan imparts much more gentle acceleration to a much larger and cooler jet. Though the jet from the core is at least as hot and fast-moving as that from a turbojet, this is only a minor part of the total. The cool surrounding stream of fan air blankets the noise from the core jet, and the reduced mean jet velocity results in considerably higher propulsive efficiency. With the 125 this would mean an increase in range of some 60 per cent for the same fuel burn and, as a bonus, noise problems and the need for heavy and inefficient silencing nozzles could probably be forgotten, at least for many years.

Rolls-Royce, from the start the established engine supplier, had been the world pioneer of turbofan engines, but unfortunately its Bristol Engine Division had been unable to do more than draw successors to

the Viper on paper. By the time the need for such an engine had become obvious, in about 1971, the company had plunged into receivership. For the next several years every penny spent on research and new design was looked at very keenly. But the oil crisis of 1973-74 made the demand for a new engine in the 5,000 lb class imperative, and Bristol Division announced that it was working on a project designated the RB.401.

As initially conceived, this engine was seen as a modern successor to the Viper in both the executive jet and advanced trainer markets. Incorporating components already proved in company research programmes, the first actual engine to be built, an RB.401-06, was first run on 21 December 1975. Unfortunately this was too late for the re-engined 125. Moreover, Rolls-Royce went on to develop a refined engine, the RB.401-07, specifically for the executive jet market. With a design rating of 5,540 lb thrust combined with outstanding fuel efficiency (significantly better than any other engine in this power class in the

The first 125-700, G-BFAN was rolled out at the Chester factory on 21 June 1976. Technically it was an F600 and in later years, during its life as the British Aerospace company "hack", the "700" designation on the side of the aircraft was changed to reflect this.

world) the -07 engine would probably have been ideal for the new 125. Sadly, the improved engine did not run until November 1977, by which time the re-engined 125 was already in production. Rolls-Royce knew that it had a potential worldwide winner in the RB.401 and proposed going ahead in collaboration with Pratt & Whitney Canada, but eventually, in 1984, the whole project was abandoned. (But Pratt & Whitney Canada then stepped in with its own engine which, as described in Chapter 11, was selected for the Hawker 1000.)

Hawker Siddeley's engine installation group at Hatfield, under Dick Pinder, actually resumed the study of available turbofan engines in

1972-3, before the extra inducement of the oil crisis. Though there were many projects, there were really only three suitable engines in existence. The General Electric CF700 aft-fan engine had been used for many years on the Falcon 20. It had ceased to be a really attractive choice, being representative of 1960s technology. On the other hand, Garrett, parent of AiResearch, once the West Coast 125 distributor, had a division at Phoenix, Arizona, which built very robust and competitive aircraft engines; it was soon to be renamed the Garrett Turbine Engine Company, and today is the Garrett Division of AlliedSignal, an industrial giant. The Phoenix team could offer two engines. The ATF3, which had been developed mainly under US Air Force contract as the F104, was rated at 5,050 lb. It was a complicated three-shaft engine with a double-reverse-flow layout and several unusual features, but on paper it seemed to be a good performer. The main problem was that the ATF3 had no civil application. (Later, in May 1976, it was selected by Dassault-Breguet to power new and existing versions of the Falcon 20, but prior to this Garrett had no commitment to certificate the ATF3 for civil operation.)

This made Hawker Siddeley look especially closely at the second Garrett engine, the TFE731. Announced in April 1969, this engine was specifically intended to replace turbojets in business jets and give them a US coast-to-coast range. It was a neat engine, but with the unusual feature of a geared fan. Visually the engine was dominated by the bypass duct for the fan air, with an outer diameter of about 30 inches. Behind this projected the core, with a combustion chamber of the annular reverse-flow type. Snuggled in the centre of this was the HP spool comprising a centrifugal compressor driven by a turbine very close-coupled (about 4 inches) behind it. Down the centre of the HP spool ran the drive shaft of the LP spool, linking the three-stage turbine at the back to the LP compressor and fan at the front. The four-stage LP compressor was driven directly, as is usual, but the rotational speed would have been too great for the 28-inch fan and so the latter was driven via a planetary-type reduction gear. A critic could say that reduction gears are just what jet engines try to get rid of, but in the

TFE731 the speed-reducing drive quickly proved its worth and demonstrated high reliability.

The gearbox played a central role in giving the engine flexibility, with good efficiency anywhere from the airfield circuit to cruising at 40,000 feet. The engine had demonstrated good specific fuel consumption (typically about half that of the Viper), low noise and lack of visible smoke. The dry weight of about 725 lb was actually significantly less than that of the Viper, which meant that to preserve the aircraft centre of gravity the TFE731 could be installed further aft, making the cabin even quieter. Altogether the 731 seemed to have hardly any minuses and many pluses, so, with a last wistful look at the RB.401, Hawker Siddeley – like several business jet builders before it and even more since – decided to "go Garrett". The decision was taken in mid-1975, but to avoid hitting sales of the already depressed Series 600 no announcement was made until, on 12 May 1976, the world was told about the forthcoming 125 Series 700.

The company demonstrator Series 700B, with appropriate registration, photographed off the Welsh coast not far from the Chester factory.

Heading towards 500...

The 400th 125 sale was celebrated at the Chester factory on 20 April 1978 with this line up of visiting customers' aircraft. G-BEFZ, the third aircraft away from the camera, was the first true Series 700. Nearest the camera is the 125-400B belonging to J.C. Bamford, whose striking colour scheme is noted in chapter 6.

The 400th aircraft went to J.A. Jones Company of Charlotte, North Carolina, at that time described as being one of the top 25 construction companies worldwide.

Exports, some 80 per cent of 125 sales, now amounted to £145 million.

At the ceremony, on which date 404 sales had actually been recorded, Leslie Tuck, then President of British Aerospace Inc., noted that orders were being taken at the rate of one per week, and that BAe planned to produce 40 125s in 1978, at an accelerating rate.

Some of the men that made it happen in the 1970s. Left to right: Percy Edwards, Production Director; Jack Garston, Chester General Manager; Jim Thorne, Hatfield-Chester Divisional Chairman; Johnny Johnstone, Marketing Director.

The earliest and most experienced TFE731 was the Dash-2 series of engines, used in such aircraft as the Falcon 10 and Learjet 35/36. This engine, at about 3,500 lb, was not powerful enough, especially since a turbofan gives proportionately less thrust than a turbojet in high-speed cruising flight. But in 1972 Garrett had begun developing a slightly more powerful version, the TFE731-3, to be rated at 3,700 lb. This engine was no bigger or heavier than the 731-2, and its specifics were only very slightly higher because of its increased turbine entry temperature. It was certificated in 1974 and quickly found many customers, one of whom was Hawker Siddeley. With a bypass ratio of 2.79, the engine for the 125-700 is designated TFE731-3R-1H ,

With so many improvements already incorporated in the 125, not a great deal had to be done in developing the Series 700 beyond the change of engine (which, inevitably, required changes to the structure and systems). Nevertheless, Collins had developed a completely new AFCS (automatic flight control system) and, as this was clearly representative of superior technology, it was adopted from the outset. In addition, numerous mostly fairly minor changes were introduced to reduce drag yet again, and improve efficiency and appearance.

Though the engines were mounted further aft than before, the pylon position was unchanged. Each pylon was reduced in depth by about 25 per cent, but exceptional care was taken to ensure the highest possible fail-safe or safe-life qualities, even after damage to the mounting structure or loss of a fan blade. The actual engine mounts were quite different from those used in the Viper, but airframe changes were held to a minimum.

To keep the cost down, the task of designing and manufacturing the nacelles (pods) was awarded to Grumman Aerospace, of Bethpage, New York, which had a good reputation as a specialist pod design and production company. Despite the much greater inlet diameter, which makes all fan-engined 125s instantly identifiable, the overall pod size and weight were, if anything, reduced. There was no longer any need for

a noise-suppressing nozzle, but two years into the Series 700 programme (a year after first flight) Aeronca cascade-type thrust reversers were offered as a customer option, but never used. The intake deicing system was simple, and integral with the nose cowl and pod, and engine fire protection was enhanced.

Early brochures on the Series 700 made no mention of significant changes to the engine controls, fuel system and several other items which, in the production aircraft, did incorporate big advances. For example, the new engines were arranged to be controlled partly by the traditional hydro-mechanical system but augmented by electronic fuel-flow computers, with switchable manual reversion. This combination of fuel controls provided features beyond those normally found in engines of the 4,000 lb thrust class. Also engine speed (rpm) of either the LP (fan) or HP spool could be automatically synchronised in flight, to avoid obtrusive low-frequency beats which could be noticed in the cabin.

A very important addition also not mentioned in the first brochures was APR (automatic performance reserve). As in some much larger aircraft, APR enables the power of either engine to be increased to a level above the normal maximum rating in the event of any failure or unlikely transient fault in the other engine. The system was designed to comprise an APR control unit, an event counter and two push-on/push-off cockpit switches. The two engine fuel computers are set to control at the APR rating, but in normal operation the APR control unit trims down the fuel flow to give the normal takeoff power. When the system is armed, either by loss of thrust from one engine or by selection of override,

the APR control unit is triggered to permit fuel flow in the remaining engine to rise to the APR level.

A bonus in the new engine was a heat exchanger, heated by scavenge oil, to heat the incoming fuel. As a result, the methyl-alcohol fuel-filter deicing system, which had been a feature of all previous 125s, was no longer needed. However the methanol tank was retained because the liquid was still needed as a standby alternative to the cockpit windscreen deicing system.

The Series 700 was planned with no changes to the fuel system other than minor improvements to the overwing fuelling and the improved

filter deicing. At a late stage, however, and reflecting the suggestions of several customers, provision was made for pressure fuelling. This enabled the entire system to be filled or defuelled under the control of a panel in the entrance vestibule. The time required to fill the system from empty was reduced from over 20 minutes to only ten. The original gravity filling system was retained, but was simplified. Unlike the arrangement in the Series 1, the baffle ribs in the Series 700 incorporated simple freely hinged valves to allow fuel to flow inboard towards the fuselage but not in the opposite direction. Another change was to introduce a smaller filler cap, giving an improved upper-surface wing profile, allowing the small vortex generators at the leading edge to be deleted.

Though there was no explicit requirement to alter the electrical system, hydraulics or air conditioning, all three needed some changes because of the completely different drive pads on the TFE731 engine.

Whereas on the Series 600 aircraft the engines are toed outwards slightly, on the Series 700 they are installed parallel to the aircraft centreline. This slightly improves efficiency in cruising flight, but at the cost of roughly a 50 per cent increase in asymmetric yawing moment in the engine-out case. Accordingly, the automatic rudder-bias system was duplicated.

One of the more important advances in the Series 700 concerned the automatic flight control system (AFCS). From almost the start of the story the AFCS had – at least in the aircraft for the US market – been a Collins contribution. The association of the Cedar Rapids, Iowa, company had been most fruitful, and in the mid-1970s Collins introduced a new "state of the art" AFCS for the corporate jet market which became available at exactly the right time for the 125-700. It will be recalled that no autopilot was fitted to some of the earliest 125s, and such equipment was by no means taken for granted. By the 1970s things had changed. Mike Goodfellow, for many years the 125 project test pilot, commented, "Autopilots are not bolt-on goodies anymore". By

A 125-700 in service with the RAF, under the designation C.C. Mk 3, photographed at its Northolt base. Since this photo was taken all of the RAF's 125s have been fitted with electronic countermeasures.

this time customers expected a complete AFCS, comprising autopilot, flight director(s) and couplers linking the flight-control system of the aircraft with the air-data system, ILS and possibly other sensor inputs.

Of course, improvements to the 125 have usually been the result of years of planning. Garrett had talked with Hawker Siddeley for several years before it came up with a suitable engine. In the same way, Collins had spent years talking about upgraded avionics, and these came to a head in 1974 when the company presented proposals for a new AFCS to Peter Cedervall, Chief Designer 125, and Charles Caliendi, Chief Systems Engineer. The design proposals were completed in September 1975. Harry Passman, Collins Vice President for General Aviation, made a final presentation, and the new system, the FCS-80, was adopted for the Series 700.

The FCS-80 three-axis AFCS can guide the 125 throughout its en-route and approach phases. TCS (touch control steering) enables the pilot to make small changes to the flight path even with air-data modes engaged. Hatfield's Chief Auto-controls Engineer, Bob McManus, supplied the Collins engineering team, led by Dr Gordon Neal, with extensive data describing the predicted behaviour of the Series 700 before the actual aircraft existed. The flight characteristics of an aircraft vary with weight, speed, centre of gravity position, altitude and configuration. Dr Neal used complex simulations to match the autopilot to the aircraft. Mike Goodfellow fed in many suggestions from the pilot's viewpoint, and Collins assigned two of its staff based at its offices in England full time to the Series 700 programme, and also built a $50,000 FCS-80 test station. At about the time the Series 700 prototype made its maiden flight, in mid-1976, prototype units began test flying in the Collins Sabreliner 60 testbed. When the first 125-700 production aircraft flew it had the complete system installed, and it worked perfectly.

Numerous minor changes were made in the Series 700 to give a smoother exterior. The belly skid was encased in a glassfibre fairing giving an improved aerodynamic shape. The lower airbrakes were redesigned with the integral castellations along the leading edge replaced by internal castellations which are concealed when the surface is closed. This change also permitted the trailing edge of the main wing skin ahead of the brake to be straightened.

Over the years Hawker interior designs have been virtually limitless. This is a themed one, in a Series 700, for a Middle Eastern customer.

Changes to the fuselage were varied. The ventral fin was enlarged to improve directional stability, and the material changed to glassfibre. The ventral trough housing hydraulic lines beneath the forward fuselage was reprofiled to fair in the forward skid pad, which on the Series 600 protruded beneath the trough. The twin ADF loop antennas were housed in a single long fairing, and a fairing was added over the housed windscreen wipers. Throughout the structure mushroom-head external rivets were replaced by the lower-drag countersunk type.

In addition to all these and other upgrades, Hawker Siddeley responded to ever-increasing customer expectancy of devices that had not even been thought of when the 125 story began. In addition to the comprehensive standard "package" of avionic equipment, the new model was equipped from the outset for such additional options as a Global GNS-500A VLF/Omega navigation system, Sundstrand FB-542B FDR (flight data recorder), Fairchild A-100 CVR (cockpit voice recorder), dual Collins NCS-31 digital frequency management systems and a GPWS (ground-proximity warning system).

In early 1976, however, the immediate task was to get a TFE731-engined aircraft into the air as soon as possible in order to measure its performance and allay any fears that the new turbofans might not be sufficiently powerful. Especially in the hot-and-high airfield case there were nagging doubts regarding the ability of the Series 700 to operate at the hoped-for MTO weight of 25,500 lb. Coupled with the fact that the Series 600 was expected to remain appreciably cheaper than the new model, it was expected that both versions would continue in production side by side.

To fly the new engines the second Series 600B demonstrator, the company's G-AZHS, was put back into the Chester factory and brought as closely as possible up to Series 700 standard. Strictly speaking, it remained a 125-F600, the prefix "F" being subsequently used to identify re-engined (F for fan) aircraft. The Series 700 was announced on 12 May 1976. On 21 June the re-engined aircraft was rolled out from Chester, resplendent in a particularly outstanding new colour scheme and with the appropriate new registration G-BFAN. It made its first flight as a Series 700 on 28 June in the hands of Mike Goodfellow, later to be Chief Test Pilot at Hatfield.

Even that first flight alone served to confirm that the TFE731 worked as advertised, that there was a dramatic reduction in noise – at all times, even including taxiing – and that fuel flow measures were at least as good as everyone's best hopes. By August 1976 all basic performance had been measured, flutter had been cleared to the design limits, and the first series of precision measures of fuel consumption had been made over a range of altitudes and speeds. After its appearance at the Farnborough Air Show in September, G-BFAN was readied for tropical trials, which were flown by Mike Goodfellow in early 1977 from Nairobi (5,000 feet and 25°C), Wilson Airport, Embakasi, Malindi and Mombasa, all in Kenya. A total of 37 takeoffs were measured, most with simulated engine failure at V_1, with 44 single-engine climbs to altitudes up to 25,000 feet. At Malindi a section of grass strip was used with a total length of 2,500 feet; in a period of one hour each engine was started here six times on the nickel-cadmium batteries, G-BFAN having no APU.

Noise measures had been planned at Cranfield in the UK in the autumn of 1976, but had to be abandoned because of very bad weather and the need to get ready for tropical trials. They were eventually done at Granada in Spain, using eight measuring sites manned by 18 engineers

Loo with a view. A number of operators elected for murals on the rear bulkhead of the toilet compartment.

in order to comply with the different requirements of both FAR Part 36 and BCAR Section N.

By May 1977 the new aircraft had been certificated by both the UK and US authorities, with excellent results. Under the existing requirements the limit for sideline noise was 102 EPNdB; the achieved level was 88.9 EPNdB under FAR 36 measures and 87.4 EPNdB under BCARs; takeoff noise (limit 93 EPNdB) was measured at 87.6/83.6 EPNdB under the two systems; and approach noise (limit 102 EPNdB) was measured at 96.3/95.9 EPNdB. The FAR 36 figures were also well inside the more stringent requirements published by the FAA for future aircraft, showing a useful margin for later development.

Altogether, the nine months which followed the first flight of the Series 700 prototype in June 1976 were the biggest turnaround in the history of the 125, and resulted in a total change in outlook. In the summer of 1976 there had for two years been what is sometimes called "a bathtub", a time of depressed sales and uneconomically slow production. There were twelve unsold 125-600s, and for the future there was a 125-700 which looked like being much more expensive and possibly lacking in hot-and-high performance. However, by the spring of 1977 every Series 600 had been sold, the price differential between it and the Series 700 had turned out to be small, the new aircraft's flight performance was in almost all respects well beyond prediction and – before any real Series 700 demonstrator was available – it was selling like the proverbial hot cakes.

As shown in the specifications, give or take a bit, the change in engines, with no change in fuel capacity, had resulted in a range increase of 1,000 miles! George Robson, Garrett's TFE731 Sales Manager for Britain, said, "The first reaction of pilots who have not been used to our engines is the quietness, and they can't believe the fuel flow. After several flights, when they get accustomed to so little noise, they start complaining of some minor buzz somewhere which with previous engines they would never have heard." Another telling confirmation of the difference in fuel burn was the early discovery that the Series 700 cruising at 35,000 feet burned fuel at a lower rate than the Series 600 when taxiing!

The arrival of the Series 700 in 1976 went a very long way towards meeting the needs of customers who had thought the 600 not fully

500 achieved!!

To commemorate the 500th sale a "fly-in" was arranged at Chester, with customer aircraft being parked in an appropriate layout.

The celebration, held at Chester on 29 October 1980, was attended by Sir Austin Pearce, Chairman of British Aerospace. He noted the possibility of choosing a new engine as an alternative to the RB.401 for the next 125 variant, and, looking even farther ahead, was quoted as saying: "The current thinking is that there should be a new design, but I believe the challenge to our engineers is to see if something more can be done to the HS 125 before we go to a new design."

The 499th and 500th 125s went to Manufacturers Hanover Corporation of New York, and the 500th was the 300th to be sold in the United States. Exactly four years since the 125-700 had made its maiden flight, this was the 142nd Series 700 to be ordered.

Total export sales in then-current values were put by BAe at "more than £400 million". The (anonymous) salesman's "optimistic" forecast of 500 sales *(see page 8)*, had been achieved in just over 18 years from the prototype's first flight on 13 August 1962.

adequate. On the other hand, some customers had spent some time on the verge of signing for earlier versions. One was Shell, at that time still managed by Douglas Bader, which after using earlier versions for years, had spent many months arguing over whether the 600 was worth the extra price in comparison with the Series 400. Then, as the contract documents were being prepared, Shell delayed the announcement for nearly two weeks. Suddenly, at a reunion of former Shell overseas engineering staff, the announcement was made: not the 400 or 600, but three 700s! But this pales into insignificance compared with the Government of Algeria. It took 13 years from the initial contract for an early 125 to the actual delivery of a Series 700 for flight inspection of navigation aids. At least the aircraft, registered 7T-VCW, operated by the Etablissement National pour l'Exploitation Météorologique et Aéronautique (ENEMA), became one of the best-looking and most fully-equipped flight inspection aircraft in the air.

Quite apart from flight inspection, several customers have studied special role fits to the 125, not excluding weapons. For survey purposes single and twin centreline cameras could be fitted, and Hawker Siddeley even test-flew a gigantic blister housing a vertical camera mounted on the door. Another option was the 125 Protector, fully equipped for maritime surveillance in the EEZ (exclusive economic zone).

Some potential customers certainly had more belligerent intentions. Instead of merely taking photos of transgressing vessels, the Chilean Air Force wanted an anti-ship missile firing capability – which, incidentally, would have presented no problems. And the Italian Coast Guard were so aware that it was actually engaged in a war against the Mafia that it studied a Series 700B with underwing bomb racks and a multi-barrel "Gatling Gun" in the nose! On a more peaceful note, all recent versions of 125 can be cleared to deploy the Flight Refuelling Rushton target from an underwing pylon.

Some of the most interesting, if not bizarre, stories come out of Africa. When the first of two 700Bs ordered by the government of Nigeria arrived at Lagos, the customer refused to accept it because it had apparently had a spell cast over it during its previous refuelling stop in a certain other African country. That certainly caused the contracts team some problems!

In contrast, a customer from another part of the world believed in mixing business with pleasure. He had mirrors at each end of the cabin, and, we are told, he usually had five women, one with an attaché case chained to her wrist. One assumes that the case held petty cash. There is also the story of the Hawker Siddeley sales representative in Saudi Arabia who was intrigued at the seemingly endless piles of big sacks being unloaded from a battered old truck and put aboard a 125. He asked what the sacks contained only to be indignantly told "Banknotes".

Chartag, which had been the first customer for the 125, decided after 18 years of successful operation with its Series 1 to buy a 700B. In 1982 its Chief Pilot, Captain Alex Federer, said, "We have come to depend on the 125's high degree of reliability, and the manufacturer's 24-hour product support service. Our new 700B has already been to Johannesburg, Washington DC and Sao Paulo. We took with us no spares whatever, and experienced no hitches, snags or delays"

E.P. Taylor, a famed Canadian racehorse owner, bought a 700 and sent his chief pilot to Hatfield to collect it. With the paperwork complete, the customer pilot said he might as well be off. Hatfield test pilot Chris Capper was somewhat startled, and explained there was quite a long procedure of briefings, instruction and a check flight. The customer pilot said, "The 125 has a better reputation than you make out", got in and flew to Canada leaving Capper ruefully to observe, "Everyone's entitled to a test drive".

When the Trust House Forte hotel group bought a Series 700, Lord Forte's sister went to Chester, and her team certainly did have a test drive. Rex Griffiths then asked if she would like a tour of Chester. She replied, "Do we have any hotels here?" They set off to tour the local THF hotels and went first to the Queen Hotel. Desperate to warn the staff, the chauffeur rushed into the foyer – but Lord Forte's sister was quicker! In seconds she had noticed numerous shortcomings, but nobody was fired: instead she ordered new furnishing fabrics. Next stop was the Post House. Of course, they had already got the message and the senior staff met her on the steps with bunches of roses!

One of the last customers to buy the Series 700 was Kuwait Airways, which acquired two aircraft for VIP charter and air ambulance work. When Kuwait was invaded by Iraq in 1990 the two aircraft, along with most of the Kuwait Airways fleet, were seized and taken back to Baghdad by Saddam Hussein's forces. It was assumed that the two 125s were destroyed in the subsequent bombing of Baghdad. However, after the conflict, Kuwait Airways heard from the United Nations that one of its missing 125s was intact and might be recoverable. A hastily assembled team from British Aerospace and Magec Aviation, together with a couple of bomb-disposal experts were despatched to Baghdad and located the intact 125, YI-AKG. (They also found the other aircraft but it was on its back and blown apart by bombs.) The intact aircraft had been repainted in Iraqi Airways colours, and in spite of some minor damage, and signs of severe neglect, it was declared safe to fly back to Kuwait City, albeit with the undercarriage down. It was subsequently believed that the aircraft had been hidden in a wood near to Saddam Hussein's palace as

a means of escape should the President have been forced to flee the country!

In the crucial US market there was no doubt whatever that the Series 700 was what a lot of people had been waiting for. In May 1977, Les Tuck, Executive Vice President of Hawker Siddeley Inc in Washington, said, "Since it was announced a year ago the response has been beyond anything we thought possible. Already eleven have been sold in North America, and no one here has even seen it yet. We announced the 700 when the economy was still recovering and although so far we have had to sell through brochures, we have had no problems at all. But there is

This 700, one of two seized by Iraqi forces from Kuwait Airways and re-painted, was safely recovered from Baghdad after the Gulf conflict…

...this one was not.

an enormous backlog of many, many potential customers who take the view that before they buy it they want to touch it".

The first production Series 700, and the first aircraft actually representative of the upgraded aircraft, again started a new sequence of constructor's numbers, being 257001, registration G-BEFZ: a 700B it flew for the first time on 8 November 1976. By 1978 the new model was coming off the Chester line at an increased rate. UK and US certification had been received in April and May 1977, respectively, with French approval following in early-1978. By this time the improved performance figures had been fully evaluated. The original estimate for range with six passengers of 2,290 nautical miles was increased to 2,340, 2,420 and then to 2,660 nautical miles, well beyond anything possible with rivals in the same cabin size and price class. One slogan coined at

the time was that the Series 700 was "a six-hour aeroplane with six-hour comfort". In the winter of 1977-78 new flight manuals for the 125-700 were issued, reflecting a considerable improvement in takeoff performance, especially from WAT-limited (weight/altitude/temperature) airfields. From such difficult runways the revised figures permitted a weight increase of up to 900 lb. and range increases of well over 200 nautical miles.

Transformed by the change in engine, the Series 700 proved to be by far the most successful sub-type of 125 so far. It kept production at an encouraging rate from 1978 until 1983, by which time 215 had been sold. They were still identified as 700A and 700B aircraft, though this ceased to mark any major engineering difference. For various reasons, the "British" or "rest of the world" B aircraft had over the years been brought up in standard to be virtually identical to the A-series, the only real difference being that Bs were finished at Chester and As in completion centres in North America.

Another change at this time was that in April 1977, under an Act of Parliament, Hawker Siddeley Aviation had become part of a nationalised organisation called British Aerospace. In turn, this was "privatised" in 1981 and further in 1985 into today's British Aerospace plc (public limited company). The HS 125, which by now, in the US at least, was commonly called a Hawker, thus became the BAe 125.

The story of the Series 700 did not end there, however. Some years later, in 1990, with the Series 800 selling well and the new BAe 1000 under development, British Aerospace wanted to broaden its product base still further and be able to offer a lower-priced 125 to compete with the cheaper Citation III. Cessna's first mid-size cabin jet had been making major inroads into the market for a number of years. The solution, BAe believed, was to rework pre-owned Series 700s and offer them in the US market with a full manufacturer's guarantee. Suitable 700s would be bought in, their airframes and engines overhauled, a guaranteed minimum life given for lifed components, avionics updated, new interiors fitted and exteriors repainted. The work programme also included a full four-year check and inspection before delivery to the customer. The aircraft was to be marketed as a type in its own right, and the designation 700-II was selected.

It was planned that the 700-II would be priced at just under $6 million, undercutting the Citation III by some $1.5 to $2 million. As well as being cheaper, the 700-II offered greater range, larger cabin and a superior fit of standard equipment. Sperry Honeywell was brought into the programme to undertake the avionics update, and a suitable Series 700A, c/n 257059, was procured and put into Arkansas Modification Center (the BAe-owned facility at Little Rock, Arkansas, which had been acquired in 1988), for work to commence. With the BAe 1000 being marketed as the "Intercontinental" version of the 125, and the 800 as the "Transcontinental", it was decided to promote the 700-II as the "Continental Class". The 700-II was thus unveiled at the NBAA Convention in New Orleans in October 1990.

Alas, the 700-II arrived at the wrong time. The market for mid-size jets became very weak during 1990 and 1991, prices for new aircraft fell, and the cost advantage of the 700-II was seriously eroded. British Aerospace dropped the programme, and 257059 became the only aircraft to receive the "Dash II" designation.

9

The F-Series retrofits

So great were the advantages of switching to the quieter, fuel-efficient turbofan engine that many operators of older 125s began to enquire about the possibility of fitting the new engines in their aircraft. For a while, between about 1981 and 1984, this became quite an important business. Aircraft thus converted were redesignated with the letter 'F' (for fan) preceding their series number. The conversions certainly gave a new lease of life to many 125s, and have kept them in economic operation right up to the present time.

Of course, it cuts both ways. How many of those operators might alternatively have bought new aircraft? The answer is surely, the customer is always right. Hawker Siddeley, and subsequently British Aerospace, discussed each conversion with the customer, because the amount of work involved went well beyond just bolting on a different engine.

The fact that the original Series 700 demonstrator, G-BFAN, was really an F600B, in other words a re-engined 125-600, showed that the idea of a retrofit programme was possible. Initially, however, priority on engine deliveries was given to fitting new Series 700 aircraft, not least because of the unexpectedly strong demand for them. But in 1977, when Series 700 deliveries were just beginning, the engineers at Hatfield and Chester, in between getting used to the idea of being part of what at that time was called British Aerospace Hatfield/Chester Division, completed the design of retrofit conversions for most earlier types of 125.

In the case of the Series 1, 1B and aircraft 25015 and 25069, a conversion would not really have been economic. These aircraft had a cabin pressurisation and air-conditioning system produced by de Havilland Propellers (which became part of Hawker Siddeley Dynamics), and this was wholly incompatible with the Garrett engines. It would have been possible, with advantage, to have removed the entire system out of the rear equipment bay and replace it with the Garrett-AiResearch system, together with an APU. However this would have begun to elevate the price of the conversion to a substantial fraction of that of an all-new aircraft, and in any case the aircraft involved were old and somewhat dated in many other respects. No operator thought such a conversion worthwhile.

In the case of all other 125s, with the AiResearch environmental system already fitted, a retrofit programme made a lot of sense. Many operators of existing 125s were perfectly happy with the aircraft in terms of comfort, capacity and reliability, and felt they could not justify the purchase of a Series 700. On the other hand the reduced noise and increase in range of some 50 per cent gained by changing engines were enormous advantages, and British Aerospace eventually designed and priced a series of conversions for different types of 125 which were sufficiently attractive to sell to a number of existing operators.

As the work involved was much more than just swapping over the engines, it was agreed that the retrofit programme could be handled only by either British Aerospace at Chester or by Garrett's AiResearch

A retrofitted F400B poses along with a standard 400B.

G-BFAN, the first Hawker to be truly retrofitted with turbofan engines, is shown here correctly identified as an F-600.

Aviation Co at Los Angeles. In December 1977 the two partners reached an agreement, under the terms of which AiResearch was to re-engine HS 125 Series 1A, 3A, 3A/RA, and 400A aircraft with the TFE731-3R-1H engine, while Chester would handle retrofits of the 125 Series 3B, 3B/RA, 400B and all sub-types of Series 600. Through a separate joint arrangement, two prototypes owned by Garrett were to fly to Chester for BAe to engineer and certify the aircraft. These aircraft, a Series 1A and a Series 400A, were converted at Chester during 1978, making their first flights with the Garrett engines on 14 December and 7 September, respectively. They were subsequently used by AiResearch to obtain FAA certification in early 1979. AiResearch Aviation flew its own first retrofit conversion on 15 February 1979.

In early 1978, BAe said that, "The price of the TFE731 engine modification is $1.4 million for delivery through mid-July 1979", but of course the price depended on many things, such as the sub-type of 125 involved and what items the customer specified. For example, the installation of the AiResearch GTCP-30-92C was one of the retrofit options offered to operators whose aircraft had not been fitted with an APU. Other options included new cabin trim to give a "wide body" look, better seating, a Series 700 type ("airliner style") toilet and cabin video, major updates to the flight deck, and various new avionics such as new VHF radios, and VOR/ILS, DME, and INS or VLF/Omega navigation systems.

In every case the conversion called for major surgery at the rear of the aircraft. The work included addition of a new engine beam, local reskinning, replacement of the pylons, strengthening of parts of the rear fuselage, a larger ventral fin (early 125s had none at all), many changes to the hydraulic and electrical systems, and fitting the double rudder-

Banco Do Brasil had its Series 400B retrofitted in 1980.

bias system to take care of the engine-out case.

BAe announced that, "These new TFE731-powered 125s will provide range increases from 35 to 40 per cent, and will meet all present and proposed FAR Part 36 noise requirements." In fact, the improvements were somewhat greater. As listed in the specifications, the actual range increases were often 60 per cent and in one case almost 70 per cent. There were also substantial benefits in takeoff field length, climb and maximum speed, but the biggest gains were always in range, especially from hot-and-high airfields. Put another way, the retrofit typically reduced the fuel bill for any given trip by 30 to 35 per cent, and in a time of what seemed astronomically expensive fuel this was a major factor in a customer's pricing of its overall flight operations.

By February 1981 a total of 48 aircraft had been committed for retrofit, the vast majority with AiResearch in Los Angeles. The time required to convert each aircraft had then stabilised at about six months.

A retired BAe engineer, who went to the United States to try to pick up an F-Series 125 for a waiting British customer, found that out of nine known to be available, just two were left, neither at less than $3 million. He reported, "The brokers are falling over themselves to buy refanned 400s – and these are aircraft with 16 to 20 years of service".

The RAF, which by now had a fleet of four 400s, two 600s, and six 700s, decided to retrofit all of its earlier aircraft to gain the economies of having a common engine type across the fleet, as well as the enormous benefits in fuel consumption and noise. It denoted the retrofitted aircraft by the addition of an 'A' suffix, thus the RAF's 400s became CC.Mk.1As and the 600s became CC.Mk.2As.

By September 1981 the total of retrofits had risen to 65, and BAe had also offered an additional option. Some customers, who had never owned a 125, had bought suitable secondhand aircraft which BAe Chester had then retrofitted. BAe said that, "As an alternative, BAe can now offer for sale, subject to availability, a retrofitted and updated BAe 125 that has been bought in by the company, to enable a potential customer to avoid the capitalisation required during the down-time of some six months, with the added advantage of earlier delivery".

As recorded earlier, BAe itself took advantage of the benefits of a retrofitted aircraft. The so-called Series 700 prototype, actually a 125-F600B, registered G-BFAN, had for almost a decade been used by the company as a communications aircraft. On virtually every weekday morning it flew Hatfield-Chester-Bristol-Hatfield, repeating the round trip in the reverse direction in the evening. It also often flew to Toulouse, and the author made its acquaintance on many occasions. ✈

10
The Series 800

In an attempt to predict the future of the BAe 125 the British monthly aviation magazine *Air International* wrote in its March 1981 issue:

"The success that has attended the introduction of the Series 700 – boosting sales to an average rate of one every ten days since the HS.125 was launched – demonstrates the importance of product-improvement programmes. Not surprisingly, there is already talk of a "Series 800", but British Aerospace salesmen are of the opinion that the Series 700 can hold its own for another two-three years, and are in no hurry to reach final conclusions as to the way the next version should be developed. A whole range of options is being studied: these could include a modest stretch of the fuselage accompanied by an increase in engine thrust, such as using the 4,000 lb st TFE731-5. More fundamental would be the introduction of a new wing with improved aerodynamics, the use of new engines such as the projected Rolls-Royce RB.401 or, ultimately, the development of a completely new design. What is certain, as British Aerospace Chairman Sir Austin Pearce said on the occasion of the (then recent) 125 fly-in, is that the company has as one of its foremost intentions to keep a firm grasp on its share of the business-jet market, and that production of the 125 and its successors is set to continue for many more years".

At that time the engineers at Hatfield and Chester, who included some sons and daughters of those who had worked on the original de

Havilland 125, had already decided to recommend a go-ahead on a Series 800, and knew exactly what form it should take. The British Aerospace board sanctioned the programme a month later, in April 1981, and detail design and tunnel model construction began at once, with actual wind-tunnel testing starting in July. This was important, because the new aircraft introduced major aerodynamic improvements. Metal was first cut in October 1981, and in April 1983 the first 125-800, c/n 258001, had been completed on the Chester assembly line and undergone resonance testing. It was rolled out for engine runs at the beginning of May.

There was no ceremony at that time. British Aerospace had not wished to damage the very successful marketing of the Series 700, but of course word about the impending "800" spread by word of mouth, especially among 125 operators. The first of the new breed, unpainted and with British 'Class B' registration G-5-11, made its maiden flight on 26 May 1983, when it climbed straight to 43,000 feet and was airborne for 3 hours 8 minutes. Only then did British Aerospace invite guests to the formal roll-out and announcement of the new jet on 1 June. By this time the aircraft was fully painted, bearing the US registration N800BA.

It was a beautiful day, and while a BAe 146 brought 90 guests from the Paris Air Show, another large group arrived in one of British Rail's high-speed trains (which confusingly, but on that occasion conveniently, are known as 125s, since they are designed to travel at 125 mph). Chief designer Peter Cedervall push-buttoned the hangar doors, and the sleek new jet – which really did cause a gasp of appreciation – rolled out towards the audience. Peter Cedervall then described all the new features, while Chester Chief Engineer Rex Griffiths pointed to each in turn. What the audience had never expected was that the new aircraft kept rolling, went out through the doors on the other side of the hangar and promptly took off! The media thought that was pretty good for a roll-out.

Of course, to quote another periodical, *Flight International,* "Before arriving at the 125-800, BAe's designers looked at everything from a different paint scheme to an all-new aircraft". In 1981 the Series 700 was still selling strongly, and seemed very much a modern aircraft, but in fact seven years had gone by since it was designed, and five since the first had flown. Aviation has always been a collection of fast-moving technologies, and nobody in it who wants to stay competitive can fail to

As early as 1974 the rear fuselage fairing that eventually appeared on the Hawker 800 was being developed on G-AZHS, the second prototype Series 600.

keep on updating his product, or inventing new ones. British Aerospace did study a few all-new replacements for the 125, but the advantages were not worth the enormous and expensive effort. Over the years the 125, no matter whether D.H., HS, BH or BAe, had gained a solid reputation which made it a known quantity in which customers could have confidence. An all-new aircraft would have to start from scratch, would be much more expensive to build and operate, and would almost certainly initially lack the 125's outstanding proven reliability. Not least, the aircraft that could result from reasonable modifications to the existing 125-700 was so good that an all-new design could only beat it by the odd percentage point.

Looking at the Series 800 the most obvious change over the 700 is a new cockpit windscreen, though in fact there are many equally important changes throughout the airframe. Less obvious is a totally new 'glass cockpit', redesigned rear fuselage and tail, and new outer wings giving a major increase in span. Hardly visible at all are the uprated engines which made the Series 800 possible.

The prototype 800 is prepared for engine runs. Note the spline down the centre of the windshield to house the air-blower to clear rain from the left-hand pane. In the event, it was found to be unnecessary and was omitted after the first few aircraft.

The prototype 800 showing the nose-probe, anti-spin chute housing and trailable static air pressure sensor.

The march of progress. The flight deck of the 800 compared with that on an early Series 1.

From this distance in time Garrett, today AlliedSignal, might not argue with a BAe engineer who said, "At the beginning, in 1977-78, Garrett was almost a disaster. It didn't know the meaning of 'support'. The whole Series 700 engine operation was conducted on a shoestring until one marvellous day when we managed to get a spare engine delivered to Heathrow. Then, quite quickly, Garrett was transformed. The TFE731 became a fine engine, we got support from Phoenix which became first good and then excellent, and since then we've never looked back".

By having the right product at the right time, Garrett has scored a global smash hit with the TFE731. By the mid-1990s more than 7,700 had been sold, and are currently powering some 3,100 civilian and military aircraft around the world. As with aircraft, successful engines have to keep getting better, and Garrett concluded an agreement with British Aerospace in 1981 for a growth version, designated TFE731-5R-1H. This was one of several variants of the Dash 5 engine, the main feature of which is an uprated LP spool. The fan was totally redesigned, enlarged, and moved forward, almost everything ahead of the axial compressor also being redesigned. Fan airflow went up from 118 to 143 lb/sec, bypass ratio being increased from 2.79 to 3.48. The LP turbine was also completely new, the three-stage unit being derived from the NASA QCGAT (quiet clean general-aviation turbofan) programme. Its increased shaft power was transmitted via a redesigned reduction gearbox.

Compared with the TFE731-3 engine, the Dash-5 was uprated from 3,700 to 4,300 lb, with reduced specific fuel consumption. Thanks to the bigger fan the noise spectra were if anything improved, and visible smoke emissions remained near zero. Inevitably, engine dry weight increased, from a brochure figure of 758 lb to 852 lb, and the small increase in length and overall diameter necessitated the design of a new pod, though very similar to that of the Series 700 aircraft, Grumman (now Northrop-Grumman) remaining the supplier.

This Hawker 800, operated by the Government of Queensland, Australia, demonstrates the aircraft's rough-field capability.

No thrust reverser was fitted at first, but British Aerospace stated that a reverser would be offered as a post-certification option. The chosen reverser was a target type, produced by the Dee Howard Company, of San Antonio, Texas. The TFE731-5 was FAA-certificated in November 1983.

To take full advantage of the uprated engine numerous changes were made to the airframe and systems, of which the largest was to fit completely new outer wings which increase wingspan by 4 feet 6 inches. Outboard of Rib 10 the structure is wholly new; inboard of Rib 10 it is strengthened. The main reason for this change was to reduce the lift-dependent (induced) drag in all phases of flight. This improves overall aerodynamic efficiency and also, despite a substantial increase in MTO weight, combines with the greater propulsive thrust to reduce field length and give much faster climb. The new wing also houses slightly more fuel, as described later.

Like its predecessors the Series 800 was designed for a crack-free life of at least 20,000 hours, with modest stress levels providing good fatigue and damage tolerance. All the experience of two million hours of 125

operations was incorporated in the Series 800, and designed from the start in the new outer wings. These were aerodynamically somewhat similar to the extremely efficient wings BAe and its predecessors had designed for the Airbus A300 and A310, with a sophisticated aft-loaded or "supercritical" section. The outer leading edge was drooped to retain the Series 700's level of maximum lift coefficient. To retain the Series 700's docile stalling characteristics the taper on the new outer panels was reduced, by kinking back the trailing edge, in order to maintain the original chord at the tip.

Structurally the entire wing was redesigned. The new outer panels were designed with integrally machined (cut from solid metal) ribs, giving the extremely accurate aerofoil profile needed to take advantage of the supercritical shape. Largely because of the greater precision of the profile, the M_{mo} (maximum operating Mach number) was raised from 0.78 to 0.80, and V_{mo} (maximum operating speed) from 320 knots to 335. From the twentieth Series 800, integrally machined ribs were also incorporated in the remainder of the wing, but in this case the main driver was reduced production man-hours. Greater precision of the wing profile is also reflected in successive aircraft adhering more closely to the ideal standard.

Careful detail redesign not only enabled the wing inboard of Rib 10 to bear the greater shear loads and bending moment imparted by the longer outer wings, but in many areas stresses have actually been reduced. The entire leading edge was redesigned to meet the latest birdstrike requirement, and the front spar and deicing strip extended to the new tip.

Increased span could mean more sluggish response to roll demands, and in any case the precisely contoured outer wings demanded improved ailerons. These actually have chord reduced in comparison with the ailerons of the 125-700, but their effectiveness is considerably greater. A key to their superior performance is that they are made with extreme accuracy, the skins being bonded to internal aluminium-alloy honeycomb. The new ailerons have one long-span tab each, of the servo-action geared type, that on the left aileron being manually trimmed via screwjacks. The horn balances are retained, but instead of extending forwards to form almost the entire tip, they extend only half-way across the chord, the fixed forward half being of glassfibre. These ailerons would

nevertheless preclude the addition of winglets, should anyone ever find such a move desirable.

Though basically the same size as that of the Series 700 (overall length is increased by 3 inches by a small addition in the cockpit section) the fuselage is modified in many places, and few parts remain common to those of the 125-700. The biggest change to the nose structure is the new windscreen frame structure carrying two enormous curved glazed panels. These improve forward view, meet the most severe birdstrike legislation and even increase the width of the flight deck, but the main reasons for their design were to reduce drag and cockpit noise level. The appearance also has a highly favourable effect upon marketing. Drag and noise are also reduced by eliminating the wipers, the front panels being of a stretched acrylic to which water droplets are disinclined to cling. Early Series 800s had a rain-shedding air blower on the captain's (left hand) pane to make sure, but this was never needed in flight and has now been omitted. The side windows are triple-element stretched acrylic, the rearmost pane on each side being hinged at its aft edge for communication and ventilation on the ground. The extra 3 inches of cockpit length was added to enable the seats to be pushed further back for greater comfort on long journeys; it also improves access to the circuit breakers. Structurally, the addition is on the front of the centre fuselage.

The combination of increased operating altitudes, calling for greater pressure differentials, and greater landing weight, demanded strengthening throughout the centre fuselage. The gauge of the top skin panel and the two bottom stringers was increased, some frames were strengthened, four new frames were added in the neighbourhood of the wing box, and the wing/fuselage fittings were strengthened. Similarly, the rear fuselage and tail structure was redesigned to bear the increased air loads, and the engine mounting beam was increased in strength. The fin was extended forwards so that its leading edge passed in front of the leading edge of the horizontal tail instead of behind it. Structurally the extra fin leading edge is made of glassfibre and houses an HF antenna, eliminating once and for all the need for any external antenna wires. The setting angle of the fixed horizontal tailplane was reduced for aerodynamic reasons, and the upper fin (called overfin in earlier 125s) was redesigned.

Major changes to the rear end resulted from modification of the fuel system. The dorsal tank, whose 50 gallons had often not been thought worth the extra system complexity, was deleted. This enabled the fin dorsal fairing to be reduced in size and improved in shape, and the HF antenna tuner was located where the tank had been. Even bigger changes took place on the underside, where the ventral fuel tank was replaced by a completely new tank which, though housing appreciably more fuel, actually reduces aerodynamic drag. This tank is wider and longer, and is faired into the rear fuselage to give a mild "double bubble" appearance. It incorporates within itself the bumper structure for wheels-up landings, faired under the rear end of the glassfibre centreline skid. At the aft end of the ventral tank are the repositioned gravity filler and pressure-fuelling connection. Immediately to the rear is a new glassfibre fairing, carrying the oxygen charging point and covering the redesigned rear bumper and jacking point. This leads to the glassfibre tailcone, with a vent grille, which despite a stumpy appearance gives minimal drag. Just ahead of it on the right side is the ground-power receptacle. The ventral fin is eliminated.

A major change to the flying-controls system was the addition of what the engineers call a stall-identification system, better (if colloquially) known as a stick pusher. It is activated from AOA (angle of attack) vanes on each side of the nose and static-pressure sensing ports under each wing. The three-channel warning system indicates approach to the stall, shaking the pilots' yokes. If the approach to the stall exceeds a predetermined rate the identification system fires the hydraulic stick pusher to initiate a nose-down pitching moment. This system was certainly not demanded by any degradation in stalling qualities – quite the reverse – but is increasingly viewed favourably by certification authorities.

The only other significant airframe change was to fit sequenced doors to the nose landing gear. Previously the doors had remained open whenever the nose gear was extended. The new doors remain closed at all times except when the gear is actually cycling (retracting or extending).

REGA developed a special craneage system for loading stretchers into its two dedicated air-ambulance Hawker 800s.

To match the increased weights of the Series 800 the tyres were uprated to be inflated to 135 lb/sq in for the main wheels and 100 lb/sq in for the nosewheels, though for operations from airstrips of low bearing strength all tyres can be reduced in pressure to about 80 lb/sq in.

No change was deemed necessary to the double-slotted flaps, which lie inboard of the redesigned portion of the wing, but to increase drag after landing the lift dump system was modified. Upon touchdown, selection of the cockpit airbrake lever to the lift-dump position immediately opens both airbrakes fully, the upper going to 47 degrees and the lower to 75 degrees. The same selection automatically depresses the flaps beyond their 45 degrees landing setting to a new 75 degrees position. This was found to be "highly effective in cutting landing roll – deceleration on very slippery surfaces is improved by 50 per cent over normal braking and aerodynamic drag".

...and on towards 1000

The business aircraft market in particular and the world's financial state in general changed markedly in the 1980s, and it took almost eight years from the announcement of the 500th sale (Chapter 8) until British Aerospace could celebrate the next 125 production milestone – the 700th sale *(right)*, on 14 July 1988. An order for three 125-800s from the Williams Companies of the US brought up the landmark, and the 125 was by now the best-selling British civil jet aircraft.

Total exports, in current values, were now put at £1.5 billion.

Meanwhile, on 24 October 1987 and almost four-and-a-half years after the variant's first flight, British Aerospace had marked the 100th sale of the Series 800, this particular aircraft, the 675th 125 of all variants, going to Alcan of Montreal, Canada *(below)*.

To the pilots, by far the greatest advance in the 125-800 was the flight deck. Apart from a major revision of the main and roof panels, the increased fore/aft length and the better forward visibility, the thing that immediately strikes every pilot who enters the flightdeck is that it is a modern cockpit, with an EFIS (electronic flight instrument system). The initial supplier was Collins, which, besides having almost a corner in the market for 125 communications/navigation avionics had also become – as far as sales were concerned at the time – world leader in the development of so-called "glass cockpits" in which multicolour CRT (cathode-ray tube) displays of impressive versatility take the place of large numbers of traditional electromechanical needle/dial instruments. EFIS displays make the flight deck much less cluttered and, instead of confronting the crew with large amounts of useless information (or possibly vitally needed information which is far from obvious and has to be interpreted), can be programmed to tell them anything they want to know. Furthermore, should anything untoward happen, the electronics immediately not only displays the appropriate warning messages, but, on request, can tell the crew about the malfunction in progressively greater detail.

Collins and British Aerospace worked together to define the EFIS-85 system, which though simpler than those developed by Collins for the Airbus A310 and Boeing 767, nevertheless uses identical technology and provides most of the same functions. John Wilson, a long-serving Hatfield test pilot, played a major role in the design of the 125's cockpits, and particularly that of the Series 800. As is invariably the case, the two displays in front of each pilot, replacing the ADI (attitude director indicator) and HSI (horizontal situation indicator) are called the PFD (primary flight display) and ND (navigation display). Both can be repeatedly reprogrammed in various ways, but in very general terms the PFD displays aircraft attitudes, rather like a traditional horizon, while the ND looks down from above and gives every kind of navigational information. The fifth display, just to the left of centre on the panel, is an MFD (multifunction display). Surrounding buttons enable the crew to call up many things, such as engine-start, takeoff or approach/land checklists, navigation alphanumeric data and flight plans, information on the aircraft systems, weather radar displays or navigation displays (which can also be repeated, if necessary in modified form, on one of the NDs) or anything else that can be outputted by the multifunction processor.

Following extensive research on advanced cockpits in the 1970s, British Aerospace began EFIS work in 1980, for the 146 and ATP airliners as well as the 125-800, and flew the EFIS-85 in a 125-700 at Chester in January 1983. Thus, the system ran a little later than the 125-800 itself, and it was not until the third Series 800 (referred to later) that an aircraft flew that could be termed representative of production standard. Since then, the system has given almost no trouble, because the major difficulties were overcome with wide-body airliners.

The point must be made that, for the Series 800A, BAe offered two other EFIS installations, by Sperry and Bendix, but customers automatically tend to pick the standard system, supplied by the company that is also responsible for all main avionics. Of course, the 125 had previously been an 'analogue' aircraft (that is the displays were of the counter/pointer types, and were thus driven by analogue signals). Thus the early Series 800 uses A/D (analogue to digital) converters to drive the EFIS displays. Part way through the 800 run the avionics were made all-digital, except for the ADF and transponders. The APS-80 flight-control system gave way to the APS-85, which had to be certificated on the 800B.

In developing the Series 800 – and following long discussion – no attempt was made to lengthen the cabin, which was considered at that time (1981) to be the optimum for this class of aircraft. At the same time, a very great deal could be done to improve not only the appearance of the interior but also the amount of room. Almost five inches was added to the width at shoulder height by sculpting the modular window panels around the frames. By recessing each passenger service unit (comprising fresh-air Punkah louvre, interior and reading lights, speaker and drop-out oxygen) completely within the interior trim along the upper sides of the cabin the appearance was improved and gains achieved in height and width. This "wide-body look", allied with a great range of fabrics and other customer options, resulted in a truly outstanding interior with no loss in thermal or acoustic insulation.

The standard (or rather suggested) layout for the Series 800 comprised galley and bar units on each side of the door in the entrance vestibule, a 26 cu ft baggage compartment opposite the door on the right side, large individual chairs in a club-four arrangement plus a fifth chair at the rear on the right, each facing a table, a three-seat settee (divan) at the rear on the left, a beautifully equipped toilet compartment and, beyond this, a second 26 cu ft baggage compartment. Of course there were numerous other possible arrangements, and in 1985 BAe offered a new large cabin option which extended the available length by 6 feet without altering the fuselage! This was accomplished by replacing the ventral fuel tank by an aerodynamically identical baggage pannier with a capacity of 28 cu ft or 500 lb. At a modest cost in range, typically from 2,454 nautical miles down to 2,100, this offers a further range of furnishing options for up to 14 passengers. In all cases the individual seats swivel through 180 degrees, are adjustable fore-aft and sideways,

and can be reclined and used as a bed. Some special-purpose interiors are discussed later.

After its initial demonstrations as N800BA, the first Series 800 was re-registered G-BKTF. It was not a prototype but a production aircraft; though, as noted, it had yet to receive the definitive EFIS in the cockpit. Again, though it was registered as an 800A, it received British markings and remained with British Aerospace, mainly at Hatfield, where it carried out the bulk of the Series 800 flight-test programme. Early in its career it sprouted a nose instrument probe for precise measurements of airspeed, a static drogue aft of the fin/tailplane fairing, and a large container aft of the tailcone housing a stall recovery parachute. The latter was not needed, despite the fact that G-BKTF carried out an exceptionally searching stall handling programme in all configurations.

The second Series 800, (an 800B, c/n 258002) flew less than a month after the first, on 24 June 1983. Painted all white, it was registered G-DCCC; studious readers will note this is the number 800 in Roman numerals. Its tasks were systems testing and performance evaluation, the latter including tropical testing at Sharjah and hot/high measurements at Harare in Zimbabwe. Noise measurements were made later at Casablanca. Throughout, all results were equal to or better than prediction, though addition of the stick-pusher inevitably raised the minimum flight speed – typically, at maximum landing weight, from 83 knots to 92 knots – resulting in BCAR landing field length being extended from 3,600 to 4,200 feet. This rarely causes problems.

The third aircraft, G-BKUH, was the first to be truly representative of the Series 800, with the EFIS-85 installed. This alone required an extensive test programme, and -UH also carried out natural icing trials in Canada, Greenland and Iceland. It was an 800A and it was eventually re-registered as N800BA (repeating the registration temporarily applied to 258001) and went to the USA as a demonstrator. Following 840 hours on the three aircraft ,the Series 800 was fully certificated in May 1984. The first customer to take delivery was Heron International with 258007.

This is what an air-to-air missile can do to a Hawker. Thanks to the aircraft's structural integrity, it was able to land safely, be repaired and return to service.

This striking view of a Hawker 800 was taken over the Welsh countryside, close to the aircraft's birthplace.

Before the takeover by AlliedSignal ,the original APU on the 800 was changed from the Garrett 30-92 to the Turbomach T62T-40C. The digital Collins autopilot, the first on any business jet, has already been mentioned and has performed excellently. As noted, another customer option is to replace the aft ventral tank by an aerodynamically identical rear baggage pannier.

North American completions were principally carried out by Arkansas Modification Center at Adams Field in Little Rock, Arkansas, a city that has since earned international fame as the home of President Bill Clinton. In 15 years ArkMod, as the company was known, grew from almost nothing to become a completion centre for several types of business jet. In 1988 it was bought by British Aerospace but today it is owned by Raytheon Aircraft and is still used for completion work and aircraft servicing.

Like the Series 700, the 800 was the end-product of many thousands of man-hours aimed at improving performance. One persistent critic of the 125 had been South African, Aaron Searll, who among other things thought the flat windscreens looked dated. As soon as he saw the 800 he said, "Now you've got yourselves a modern aeroplane" and promptly bought the British Aerospace demonstrator.

One of the early customers was Australian Carlton and United Breweries. This aircraft was one of the few to be boldly painted in an overtly marketing livery, advertising Fosters lager (every one of the 4,000 folk at Chester were given a can when the sale was announced). Another

One of a number of Series 800 aircraft supplied to the Royal Saudi Air Force.

such aircraft features Popeye hamburgers. But many customers are coy in the extreme. A few still suffer from the fear that ignorant stockholders will think an executive jet a mere expensive toy. A far more valid reason for anonymity is that most 125 corporate buyers operate in "the big league" where deals run into billions. It helps if competitors do not know where one's business jets happen to be at any particular time. And there is also, of course, the problem of security against various forms of threat. Business aircraft manufacturers never publish lists of customers, but if you want to find out who that completely faceless all-white Hawker belongs to, all you have to do is look up one of the unofficial, but comprehensive, lists published by the aviation enthusiasts and spotters' clubs!

Meanwhile, selling and operating 125s in Africa still continued to bring in surprises. Signing a contract in Nigeria for two Series 800s was imminent when a delay was caused by a coup which nearly toppled the government. The ringleaders were rounded up, causing more delay. As one of the coup leaders was being flown to Lagos, a fight broke out which resulted in the pilot being shot in the head and the aircraft crashing with no survivors. Africa is not an easy place to sell executive aircraft.

The 112th Series 800 was sold to Botswana and by fate it was to suffer sudden and violent attack. Delivered on 6 June 1988, it was received amidst great rejoicing and straight away embarked on crew

The Australian Elders XL group painted its 800 in the colours of one of its most popular products – Foster's lager.

training. On 8 August 1988, OK-1, as the aircraft was registered, was taking President J.K. Quett Masire and his staff to Luanda, Angola, for a meeting of Front Line States. Whilst at cruising height at 35,000 feet something catastrophic happened to the right engine. Fan blades came through the fuselage, and the steward was blown forward on to the Botswana Chief Pilot, incapacitating him. The British Aerospace pilot in the right-hand seat, Arthur Ricketts, who was on secondment supporting the new customer, took control, descended rapidly, lowered the undercarriage at 10,000 feet and finally made a successful landing at Cuito Bie, a remote strip in the African bush which, by good fortune, just "happened to be there".

Everyone was more or less uninjured, but when they looked at the aircraft they wondered if the right engine had in some way exploded like a thousand-pound bomb. There were many puzzling features. Two

days later the Angolan Government admitted what had happened. An over-eager Angolan Air Force MiG-21 pilot had fired two air-to-air missiles at the 125. One had hit the engine and blown it off the aircraft. The second, by enormous good fortune, had locked-on to the falling engine. (If it had not done so, the aircraft would have had little chance of survival). Nothing could better have demonstrated the sheer strength and survivability of the 125, which was recovered and returned to Chester for repair. Meanwhile, Botswana, impressed by the resilience of the 125, took delivery of a new Series 800, in the sure knowledge that these aircraft are hard to shoot down. After extensive repairs were completed the damaged 800 was sold on to a customer in South America, where it is still flying. ✈

This 125-800 was purchased by the Shaher Trading Company in 1986: the registration mark "4W" denotes the Yemen Arab Republic.

What might have been...

In the 1980s British Aerospace produced these two concepts. The artist's impression *(below)* is of a future supersonic business jet. Such a development was envisaged to carry 12 passengers at a speed of Mach 1.85 over distances of up to 3,800 nautical miles.

The artist's impression *(left)* shows a "datum for what might be considered as the ultimate development of the 125", according to the original caption. "BAe intends to remain competitive in the business jet market," it continued, "and will focus on developments of its existing BAe 125 Series 800.

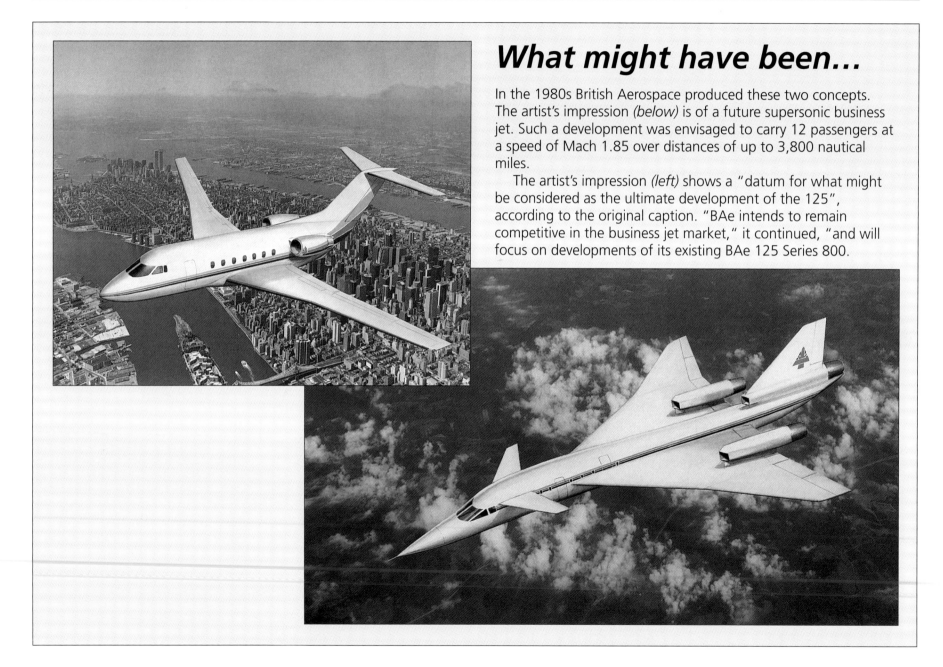

11
Special variants

A number of 800s have been equipped for special duties for which the equipment and fitting-out has cost has been as much as the basic aircraft. For example, two aircraft, HB-VIK and HB-VIL, are intensively operated by REGA, the Swiss air ambulance organisation. REGA previously owned Learjets and a Canadair Challenger, but the former were lacking in several respects. After carefully evaluating five alternatives, the two 125-800s were ordered in October 1986. Equipment includes two stretchers (loaded via an electric hoist), a leg-rest chair (as an alternative to two normal passenger seats), seats for a doctor and nurse, and a comprehensive array of monitoring and therapy instruments including an ECG monitor, defibrillator, incubator and respirator, special oxygen system, pumps for infusions and injections, and a broad range of drugs and catheters. Each aircraft is a complete flying intensive-care unit. Another unique feature is that these aircraft also have three inertial navigation systems, to full airline standard, so that the aircraft can operate completely independently of ground-based navigation aids worldwide.

Another important duty is that of flight inspection, a role for which a considerable number of 125s have been fitted-out over the years. This involves the precision inspection and calibration of such ground-based aeronautical facilities as Tacan/DME, VOR, ILS (plus marker beacons), DME, NDB, DF, VHF and UHF communications, PAR, ASR/ATCRBS and visual aids such as are used on landing approaches. To do this a flight-inspection aircraft requires additional equipment with which its position in three dimensions can always be measured with extreme accuracy. Such equipment typically includes an RTT (radio telemetry theodolite), IRU (inertial reference unit), precision barometer for pressure altitude measurement, and a forward-looking laser rangefinder.

One of the most important contracts for such aircraft was for the C-FIN (combat flight inspection and navigation) role for the US Air Force. Following detailed evaluation of all aircraft available, the 125-800 was selected in 1988. The US Air Force stated that the British aircraft possessed outstanding characteristics, superior to those of its competitors, together with a significant cost advantage. The six aircraft, having the

USAF designation C-29A, are equipped with an LTV Sierra automatic flight inspection system.

These aircraft entered service at Scott Air Force Base, Illinois, from April 1991. They replaced the T-39 and C-140, the user unit being the 1467th Facilities Checking Squadron (FCS). The 125s have proved trouble-free and user-friendly, and well able to handle the critical leg from Travis AFB, California, to Hickam AFB in Hawaii. Throughout the Gulf War five of the six C-29As were active in that theatre, flying

The P.134, one of two special variants of the 125 proposed by the Military Division of British Aerospace around 1990.

501 sorties to inspect navigation aids in Oman, Saudi Arabia, the United Arab Emirates, Egypt, Turkey, Bahrain, Qatar and finally at Kuwait City International .

On 1 October 1991 the FAA assumed all responsibility for flight inspection of military as well as civilian navigation aids throughout the United States, and the 1467th FCS was deactivated. The C-29As were transferred to a new Air Force Flight Inspection Center at the FAA's Mike Mulroney Aeronautical Center at Oklahoma City. Two of the aircraft were detached to Hawaii and Tokyo to serve Pacific facilities, with another two based at Rhein-Main AB near Frankfurt-am-Main, Germany. To reduce costs, all are now being drawn back to Oklahoma City and repainted as civil aircraft, though they remain the property of the Air Force. They are operated and maintained by the FAA, but are actually flown by combined USAF and civilian crews.

The C-29A selection had a significant influence on an order placed in August 1989 for three aircraft for the Japanese Air Self-Defense Force (JASDF) FC-X programme. This was the first time since World War 2 that any of the Japanese forces had selected a foreign aircraft that was not American. These aircraft are designated U-125, and are equipped for flight inspection. Again Sierra Research played a central role, but with Japanese participation by Kanematsu Corporation, Fuji Heavy Industries and Cornes & Co. Their equipment includes a laser altimeter under the tail whose readouts are photographed together with the "piano keys", the black/white bars on the end of the runway (which the U-125 can illuminate at night), to give a precise 3-D position on each test approach from each end of the instrumented runway. The first U-125 was handed over on 16 December 1992.

Earlier, in August 1991, the 125-800 won over tough competition from the USA and France to be selected as the future land-based SAR (search and rescue) aircraft of the JASDF. The total requirement is for 27 aircraft, designated U-125A, costing in 1991 money about US$750 million. The aircraft are being purchased by the Japanese Defense Agency in small batches on a Fiscal Year basis for delivery from 1995 to 2003 (Japanese years 5755 – 5763). They are replacing much smaller, slower and shorter-ranged MU-2s, and for the first time give a total all-weather and night search capability.

The second special variant of the 125 proposed by the Military Division of British Aerospace around 1990 was the P.135.

The U-125A required the most extensive modifications ever made to any 125, calling for the issue of some 8,500 new drawings. Very much the proverbial "quart in a pint pot", these aircraft are equipped for every kind of SAR activity short of actually alighting on the sea.

From the outset, Japanese industry has played a significant and increasing role in the programme, and eventually "green" aircraft will be flown to Japan for equipping and systems testing by Fuji Heavy Industries. Most of the mission equipment is Japanese. Toshiba provides the surveillance radar, a Texas Instruments APS-134 made under licence. Its 360-degree scanner is faired in under the leading edge of the wing. Melco supplies the FLIR (forward-looking infra-red) imager, made under licence from FLIR Systems Inc. It is packaged in a turret which can be extended through a door in the lower side of the nose, the sensor head rotating (normally slaved to the radar) linked via an ingenious twisting cable loom. The extended FLIR required the addition of a small ventral

C-29A Combat
Flight Inspection
Aircraft, six of which
were acquired by the
United States Air
Force and which are
now operated by the
FAA.

The first U-125
Flight Inspection
aircraft for the Japan
Air Self Defense
Force (JASDF)
undergoes a
traditional Shinto
blessing ceremony.

tail fin. On each side of the fuselage, ahead of the wing, is what is popularly called a "patio window" giving an optically undistorted view which extends almost directly downwards. The cabin is devoted to operator stations with a layout different from the U-125. A launcher, reloaded from inside the cabin, is provided for dropping parachute flares and sea markers, while life rafts can be dropped through the left main landing-gear well.

To drop a life raft, the aircraft lets down to 1,500 feet while a metal cover in the cabin floor over the left wheel well is progressively unsealed, its eccentric hinge cams gradually releasing cabin pressure. The cover is then opened, and the raft, contained in a circular metal can just fitting the well, is loaded and the cover closed. A run is then made with 15 degrees of flap at 150 knots to the drop point, where the undercarriage is extended, allowing the raft to drop out. It inflates on hitting the water.

The U-125A has a ZFW increased from 18,000 lb to 18,450 Ib, providing for a mission-equipment weight of 4,450 lb. Clearing the U-125A specifications and manuals was an enormous task, shared between Japanese and British establishments. Stores-release tests at simulated drop conditions was one of the last tasks carried out by the 9 feet x 7 feet wind tunnel at BAe Hatfield before it was dismantled and taken to the University of Glasgow. The live trials were a seven-days-a-week job by BAe test pilots from July to October 1994 at the Ministry of Defence establishment at West Freugh, Scotland, 320 hours being needed in 160 flights. Ground tests at speeds from 40 to 110 knots on the 230-foot water trough laid on a runway at Cranfield, England, confirmed that the water plume thrown up by the nosewheels would neither damage the radome nor be ingested to an adverse degree by the engines. An anechoic chamber in Japan checked that there would be no interference between the radar and the FLIR. Overall the trials were outstanding, several results being better than prediction.

Formal handover of the first three U-125A aircraft took place at Fuji's Utsunomiya base to the north of Tokyo on 28 February 1995. A spin-off from this very important programme is that it has enabled the 125 to be offered as a fully-equipped and extremely versatile aircraft in an international configuration which is now attracting interest in several countries.

Around 1990, the Military Division of British Aerospace at Warton worked on two projects based on the 125 designated P.134, a signals-intelligence (Sigint) platform, and P.135, a surveillance aircraft. The P.134 would have been equipped to collect, pinpoint, analyse and, if necessary, transmit in real time by secure data-link, any desired type of hostile emissions, for Elint (electronic intelligence), Radint (radar) or Comint (communications). The cabin was configured for a mission commander, Elint operator, Comint operator and Comint listener. The receivers were software-controlled and remotely programmable to cover frequencies from 20 MHz to 18 GHz. Five groups of antennas were sited to give maximum probability of intercept, with minimum airframe screening and a direction-finding accuracy better than 1 degree on most frequency bands. The system included a transportable data-link GET (Ground Entry Terminal). Endurance at optimum altitude (up to 43,000 feet) was in excess of 6.5 hours, and detection range up to 230 nautical miles was achievable. If necessary the aircraft could be equipped with a defensive warning system, including counter-measures, such as a jammer and dispensers for flares and chaff. The project got as far as a model being tested in the Hatfield wind tunnel.

An U-125A Search and Rescue aircraft for the JASDF which has a potential requirement for 27 of these aircraft.

The P.135 was again predominantly military in character and was essentially a vehicle for lifting to high altitude (above 40,000 feet) a single large and capable sensor, a synthetic aperture radar. This radar incorporated an advanced digital motion compensation technique which reduces errors caused by aircraft response to turbulence and buffet, giving essentially constant resolution over the entire stand-off range. Raw radar data are processed on board, so the operator sees a real-time image. The big ventral radome, incorporating a radar altimeter and secure downlink antenna, required a ventral tailfin to be installed. Other equipment included nose weather radar, dorsal GPS and dual ADF antennas, front and rear radar warning receivers at the top of the fin, and chaff/flare dispensers under each side of the rear fuselage. The cabin was occupied mainly by radar racking, but included an operator/analyst station, optional observer seat, toilet, galley and coat closet.

With increasing interest being shown by national governments in aircraft capable of undertaking these activities, the P.134 and P.135 concepts, suitably updated, may yet see the light of day.

* (A list of special mission roles undertaken by Hawker/125s to date can be found in Appendix 7). ✈

12

The BAe 1000

(Hawker 1000 after 1993)

When the largest member of the family was launched it was not called a 125 at all, but was for a time marketed under the name "Corporate 1000" – and more usually as the British Aerospace 1000 – to try and emphasise the differences between it and the BAe 125-800. It is the most powerful and perhaps best-looking of the 125/Hawker range, and it was designed to give trans-Atlantic range capability. Its history is far from straightforward, and has been affected by the dramatic changes in the market, the dominance of the US market (which tends to be polarised around the shorter ranges of coast-to-coast), a considerable increase in price and, not least, a failure to meet optimistic initial range forecasts. At the same time, the BAe1000 (which, as is discussed in the next chapter, became universally known as the Hawker 1000 when Raytheon acquired the programme) is unquestionably an important member of the family, loved by pilots, and which should mature as a highly competitive aircraft.

The genesis of the BAe 1000 came about in several ways. One was a straightforward 1980s study of the world business jet market and the aircraft on offer, which emphasised the way each available type was either a small-cabin short-range, or a medium-cabin medium-range, or a large-cabin long-range. There was no medium-cabin long-range. A second factor was that, when the 125 Series 700 and 800 hit the market, the number of potential customers who wanted a longer range than the 2,000 – 2,500 nautical miles that these aircraft offered could be counted

The first Hawker 1000 under construction at the Chester factory in April 1990.

125, and was to be powered by two Rolls-Royce RB.401 turbofans. This engine, an all-new design in the 5,500-lb thrust class, promised unrivalled sfc (specific fuel consumption), a target hit within two per cent on the engine's first run in November 1977. The wing was to have an advanced supercritical profile similar to that which the same designers had just created for the Airbus 310. The inner wing was shaped to give ideal flow characteristics in conjunction with the engine nacelles.

This "Series 800" promised to fly the 3,480 nautical miles London – New York sector at airline cruise speeds. Pratt & Whitney Canada took a franchise on the RB.401 and arranged to collaborate on its further development. All seemed set fair for a most successful future when, in 1984, for reasons due to US anti-trust laws rather than anything to do with the engine itself, Rolls-Royce most unfortunately "pulled the plug" and terminated the RB.401 programme.

Back in the 1970s the position was coloured by the widespread belief within what was then British Aerospace that the 125-700 was the end of the line. The launch of such rival aircraft as the Learjet 54/55 Longhorn and Cessna Citation III appeared to make the development of a trans-Atlantic 125 a risky investment in view of the very large costs involved. Accordingly, even before the RB.401 was cancelled, BAe concentrated on improving the 700 and, via a proposed 750, went ahead on the aircraft known today as the 125-800, which proved to be a worldwide success.

Nevertheless, the transatlantic (say, 3,300 – 3,500 nautical miles) objective never went away. It was always there, affecting more and more customers, and, when the various rivals failed to live up to their brochure promises, BAe began once more to study what could be done. Before Peter Cedervall retired as Chief Designer in April 1987, a complete outline design had been formulated for a 125-800I (800 Improved), with additional fuel and TFE731-5BR engines. This could nudge 3,000 nautical miles, but a few potential customers kept demanding about 500 nautical miles more than this. Moreover, there was a requirement for a longer cabin, with more seats and greater baggage capacity.

BAe formed the opinion that there was not much further stretch left in the TFE731 engine, although the -5BR continued to remain an option

The first Hawker 1000 during its ninth test flight on 11 July 1990.

on the fingers of one hand, and almost every one was in the USA. In contrast, by the late-1980s there were over 50, and a growing proportion of them were in Pacific Rim countries. A third factor is that the early 125 versions were invariably sold to first-time buyers who had wondered fearfully whether they were foolhardy to spend so much; then, having taken the plunge, they kept the aircraft for many years. Today's customers are often on their third or fourth business jet, and there are a growing number of fleet operators. An ever-greater number call for more range, and often more capacity.

British Aerospace never ceased to consider how best to respond to these factors, and in the late 1970s its ideas were encapsulated in a proposed all-new long-range business jet called the 125-800. This project was, however, unrelated to the 125-800 which was later actually built. It had a fuselage of 82 inches diameter, ten inches greater than the existing

for some time. The link between Rolls-Royce and Pratt & Whitney Canada brought Hatfield and Montreal back together (the JT12 turbojet had been the first engine considered for the 125) and discussions began on a new engine to replace the RB.401. This quickly emerged as the PW305, a turbofan with a takeoff thrust of 5,236 Ib, or 4,750 lb maintained to 25°C. Components were tested in 1986, and the first complete engine ran a year later.

This engine has a bypass ratio of 4.3, compared with about 3.4 for the TFE731-5. The single-stage fan has a diameter of 30.7 inches, and is a larger and stronger version of that fitted to the JT15D used in small business jets, with an excellent record of resistance to birdstrikes. The compressor, likewise, rests on the technology of the latest PT6 turboprops, with four axial stages followed by a centrifugal. From the latter's diffuser casing a ring of curved pipes duct the air to the annular combustor, which unlike other PWC engines is not of the reverse-flow type. The HP turbine is based on that of the PW100 turboprop family but has two stages, only the first having cooled blades. Last comes the three-stage LP turbine, for which MTU, a subsidiary of Germany's Daimler-Benz, is responsible.

Accessories are driven off the front of the HP spool via a tower shaft which passes down to the gearbox on the underside of the fan case. On the left side of the fan case a large box identifies the Dowty Smiths FADEC (full-authority digital engine control), which relieves the crew of almost every engine-management task. The cockpit power levers have such simple annotations as TAKEOFF, LR CRUISE and HS CRUISE. The pilot slips the levers into the appropriate position and the FADEC

The third Hawker 1000 in its Rover-designed paint scheme.

The Honeywell SPZ 8000 equipped flight deck of the Hawker 1000.

takes care of everything else. For example, on takeoff it commands the optimum thrust having regard to ambient temperature and pressure. Each engine also has its own self-diagnostic box with which a maintenance engineer can call up on the display such things as all engine readings, hours flown and many other factors. One factor is the number of times APR (auto performance reserve) thrust has been demanded or exceeded following real or simulated engine failure.

Not only is the PW305 more powerful than previous 125 engines but its brochure sfc is significantly lower. BAe was told that the sfc in high-speed cruise at 40,000 feet/Mach 0.8 would be 0.675, or some 16 per cent lower than for a TFE731-5. Initial TBO (time between overhauls) was set at 2,500 hours, but operators had the option of joining the ESP (Eagle service plan), offering a fixed total maintenance/overhaul

price per flight hour for the whole aircraft.

Of course, the PW305 was designed to meet existing and immediately planned standards for noise and other emissions, in most cases with a considerable margin. Thus, it needs no noise-suppressing nozzle, though its excellent noise spectrum is reduced further by advanced acoustic linings throughout the nacelle. This time the contract for the design and manufacture of the entire pod and reverser was won by Rohr, a Chula Vista (San Diego) firm needing no introduction to anyone in the airliner business. The pod is unlike that of any previous 125, and, despite a ventral bulge round the accessories, has lower drag. The aluminium target-type hydraulically-operated clamshells are hinged to paired struts normally housed in aft-projecting fairings which BAe called "stangs". This is the first time that a reverser has been standard equipment on a 125.

Another product from San Diego is the APU. The Turbomach T62-T40C8D-1 drives the same type of starter/generator as the main engines. It provides ground electrical power and air conditioning.

Having selected a new engine – in itself a bold step – BAe considered how best to obtain the desired extra cabin volume and fuel capacity. Both were achieved by redesign of the fuselage and fuselage/wing fairing. At first glance the body can be seen to incorporate plugs ahead of and behind the wing, but in fact the entire fuselage was redesigned to have the optimum structure, more efficient than one subjected to repeated stretching, and designed from the start to meet more severe requirements. The plug ahead of the wing adds 18 inches, and that behind the wing 15 inches. This increases cabin length by 13 per cent, adding an extra window on each side. Moreover, the aft end has been redesigned.

Since certification of the 125-800, FARs (US Federal Air Regulations) and JARs (the European Joint Airworthiness Requirements) have been upgraded to take into account what happens following multiple perforations of the rear pressure bulkhead by engine debris, or any other damage. Loss of cabin differential pressure must not exceed a specified rate, and a stipulated pressure differential must be maintained. The 125-800 could not quite meet this requirement, and so in the USA (but not elsewhere) this variant is restricted to a height of 41,000 feet. The Hawker 1000 was designed with a complete secondary pressure bulkhead

A typical Hawker 1000 interior.

28 inches in front of the original. This extra bulkhead is an aluminium sandwich 1.5 inches thick, so that though flat it can withstand full pressure differential. The space between the two bulkheads (which has gained an extra 5 inches of length compared with the 800) was designed as a new aft baggage compartment. Access is gained via a door in the centre of the new pressure bulkhead, and also via a new external door on the left side just in front of the engine. This external door measures 25 x 14 inches, and is of the plug type, pushing in and sliding up. To recap, the 1000 fuselage is 33 inches longer than that of the 125-800, and of this 28 inches extends the cabin and 5 inches is added to the aft baggage bay.

Beyond structural redesign for higher weights little has been done to the wing. In place of the drag-inducing fences are small vortilons, as first seen on the DC-9. These are small boundary-layer fences on the underside of the leading edge. They do nothing in cruising flight, and so cause negligible drag, but at high angles of attack they create a powerful vortex which keeps the boundary-layer attached and prevents spanwise flow out towards the wingtips. This improves lateral control, reduces stalling speed and shortens required field length.

A more obvious change is the improved wing/body fairing. Aerodynamically it is as perfect as Hatfield could make it, but it also makes possible a significant increase in fuel capacity. The long forward fairing adds 135 gallons, while the 5-inch stretch at the rear adds a further 30 gallons. This extra tankage is all integral, and the aft gravity filler has been eliminated. If filling has to be by gravity the wing fillers only are used, fuel being transferred to the fore and aft ventrals by the tank booster pumps. New JARs require cockpit indication of the fuel in every tank. The ventral tanks are thick-skinned to withstand any normal belly landing, and the Structural Dynamic Research Corporation, with long experience of analysing Formula-1 racing car crashes, produced software to show that the impact resistance of these tanks is "at least as good as that of the wing itself".

Aerodynamically, the flight controls were unaltered, but to meet new JARs the aileron and elevator circuits were redesigned to provide full control in the event of any circuit being locked inoperative by a mechanical jam. To meet this severe demand of dual redundancy, the elevator had to be split into totally independent left and right surfaces. From the 125-800 onwards it has been mandatory to have two pilots, so there should always be a properly qualified pair of hands near each yoke. Accordingly, the left yoke drives the left elevator, and the right yoke the right. The duplicate elevator linkage passes down the centreline of the fuselage below the floor in the space previously occupied by manual engine controls. Normally the elevators are joined across the centre by a torque strut. At a load level well above anything encountered in normal flight this disconnects to allow the left and right elevators to operate independently. Thus, should either circuit jam, the aircraft can be flown on that remaining, the unwanted roll effect being insignificant.

Hawker 1000.

Likewise, a jam in either aileron circuit leaves the aircraft controllable on the other. In fact, the 1000 is flyable in roll on the rudder alone but this was not considered adequate to meet the JAR requirements. A further modification is to enlarge the bullet fairing at the rear of the fin/tailplane junction. This was necessary to house the modified elevator controls.

Though the cockpit is very like that of a late-model 125-800, the avionics are almost completely new. Many customers for Series 800s selected the Honeywell (Sperry) SPZ-8000 automatic flight control system, and this is the baseline fit on the 1000. Thus, the 1000 has been a digital aircraft from the start, and this is in line with the refinement and upgrading of all the on-board avionic items. The Honeywell system uses 5 x 6-inch EFIS panel displays (compared with 5 x 5 for Collins), and the installed SPZ-8000 is roughly 25 lb lighter. The standard radar is the Honeywell (Sperry Primus) 807. The aircraft is wired for dual Honeywell (Sperry) FMZ-605 flight management systems, and dual Honeywell Laseref III laser inertial navigation systems.

Airframe changes are rounded off by the main undercarriage, which is strengthened to handle the increased weights, and a high-capacity

deicing system. The ice-detection head is of the vibrating-probe type. The TKS deicing fluid is housed in a larger tank to cater for icing lasting up to nine hours, and the fluid is expelled through porous leading-edge strips, that on the outer wing being of laser-drilled titanium. Fuselage lamps can illuminate both leading edges at night.

BAe denied that the existence of the Dassault-Breguet Falcon 900 influenced the choice of '1000' as the designation of the new aircraft. Rather did they state that bypassing '900' was due to the fact that almost every operative system was carefully redesigned. Over more than 20 years each system had been subjected to so many modifications that they had tended to become 'bitty' and overweight. In the 1000 each has been rethought from scratch. The Honeywell digital avionics require

Over a quarter of a century separates these aircraft. Shown is the second Hawker 1000 development aircraft, G-OPFC, (both it and the first 1000 confusingly actually carried Series 800 constructor's numbers), posing alongside aircraft number 9, a Series 1, built in 1964, This was operated by the Royal Aircraft Establishment, Bedford, and modified for use in the Blue Vixen radar trials. XW930 has since been disposed of for spares.

DC, and this enabled the AC system and inverters to be deleted. Each engine FADEC has four wire looms which are widely separated along the top and bottom sides of the fuselage. This was one of the features needed to enable FADEC control to be certificated without manual reversion, marking a 'first' on any business jet. The ECS (environmental control system), made by a division of AlliedSignal, incorporates a C-29A type precooler, as well as improved control and an independent supply to the cockpit.

Many customers were consulted on the required size of cabin. Of course, some demanded doubled galley facilities to provide two cooked meals several hours apart, with quality crockery, cutlery and washing-up facilities. The optimum is a galley able to store ten three-plate place settings, cook frozen food and wash up afterwards. The cabin is certificated for up to 15 passengers. Normally a smaller number is catered for, with very comfortable seats which can swivel, recline and travel to any desired stretch-out position. To cater for nine hour sectors up to 1420 litres of gaseous oxygen is carried in each of the bottles relocated in the nose.

In August 1988 BAe purchased the car maker The Rover Group plc. Hatfield invited Rover's graphic designers to come up with paint schemes for the first three 1000s to come off the Chester line, and these were finished in attractive liveries of blue or maroon. These aircraft flew on 16 June and 26 November 1990 and 23 February 1991 respectively: certification was received from the CAA on 19 October 1991 and from the FAA ten days later. Deliveries to customers began in December of that year. (The first aircraft, registration G-EXLR, standing for EXtended Long Range, made a ceremonial "first flight" from Chester on 28 June 1990, after which it landed at the BAe flight test centre at Woodford, near Manchester, from which the 1000's flight trials were carried out. The second 1000 was registered G-OPFC, in honour of Peter Cedervall, who was the 125's Chief Designer for some 20 years until his retirement in 1987. The third aircraft bore the registration G-ELRA – Extended Long Range Aircraft – and was the first to have a Series 1000 constructor's number, curiously 9003.)

These dates (for certification and first delivery) were later than planned. In part this was due to a long strike by production workers at Chester, but a contributory reason was a series of problems which, though not serious in themselves, proved difficult to identify and solve. The most intractable was a slow undulating longitudinal (pitch) one cycle per second oscillation at high Mach numbers, considerably faster than anything normally encountered in long-range cruise. The complete horizontal tail was the same as that on the 125-800, but the longer fuselage puts it 15 inches further aft, which altered the wing/tail coupling and required a slightly different tailplane incidence. The problem was that at Mach numbers between about 0.85 and the required dive demonstration limit of 0.87 shockwaves were migrating back from the tailplane to drive the leading edge of the elevator. Test pilots Peter Sedgwick, George Ellis and Tim Miller spent weeks making dangerous excursions to extreme Mach numbers, nudging total uncontrollability, before solutions were found in a narrow window of tailplane setting to meet all flight conditions between Mach 0.87 and the landing flare, whilst keeping stick forces under negative-g acceptable. A so-called "dolphin bullet" ahead of the fin/tailplane intersection was not needed, but the tailplanes did receive vortex generators on the upper surface plus a shallow wedge on the underside immediately ahead of the elevator.

During this protracted investigation the first two aircraft were undertaking the basic certification, c/n 8151 (G-EXLR) for handling and 8159 (G-OPFC) for systems and performance. Tropical trials were held at Yuma, Arizona, and noise tests at Roswell, New Mexico. It soon became apparent that the published figures for range/speed/payload were not going to be achieved. Before first flight the IFR launch estimate was approximately 2,750 nautical miles at Mach 0.77 rising to 3,230 nautical miles at Mach 0.7, with 1,200 lb payload and full reserves. Early deliveries missed this by about 500 nautical miles, and it was also found that, though there was no problem in normally cruising anywhere from Mach 0.735 to 0.8, the most fuel-efficient Mach number was 0.7. Moreover, at this speed the aircraft was unhappy, especially at high weights, and range was further spoiled by the need, at this low Mach number, for frequent power changes.

In December 1992, as will be related in Chapter 13, British Aerospace appointed a new management team led by Bill Boisture, one of the most experienced men in the business. Immediately he organised range

demonstrations with the 1000 on trans-Atlantic sectors and on triangular routes to northern Scandinavia: these established that the best range attainable was 3,070 – 3,080 nautical miles.

Of course, there were arguments over where the lost range had gone. BAe accepted that drag was slightly above prediction, and PWC admitted that the installed PW305 was slightly down on thrust and up on specifics, especially at high temperature. Quickly the Montreal engineers produced the PW305B, with several mostly minor modifications but in particular with better hot-end cooling and stiffer casings. The engines had originally been tested whilst hung from above, whereas being hung in the aircraft from the side had led to slight distortion, and with so small a core the blade tip clearances are very sensitive. The PW305B is flat rated at 5,266 lb to 15°C, giving hot-and-high performance better than the original estimates, and brochure sfc at Mach 0.8 at 40,000 feet is 0.681. In most adverse circumstances an APR of from 7 to 11 per cent increase in thrust can be obtained by letting the FADEC push the throttle through the takeoff detent. However, this is effective only above the flat-rating level.

Meanwhile, the Hatfield engineers never ceased working to improve the basic aircraft. Drag has been reduced by numerous small changes. Takeoff problems were caused mainly by the higher V_{MC} (minimum-control speed) resulting from the more powerful engine. By the simple expedient of putting a four degree kink in the jetpipes, so that instead of being directed two degrees inwards they point two degrees out, the turning moment that has to be held by the rudder is significantly reduced, with no change in fuel economy. Landing distances have been reduced by redefining the Flight Manual approach speeds as a function of the VS_{1g} (unaccelerated) stalling speeds.

Though most unwelcome, the initial shortfall in range was of little interest to most potential customers for the 1000, for whom US coast-to-coast at high-speed cruise (not under Mach 0.8) is achievement enough. No other business jet in anything remotely like the same price bracket can do this, except for (marginally) the Astra which has a much smaller and less comfortable cabin.

The 1000 has demonstrated many solid achievements. No other business jet has been required to demonstrate Mach 0.87 with either manual flight controls or a fixed tailplane. It is a good-looking aircraft which offers a most comfortable walkabout interior perfectly matched to sectors up to 3,000 nautical miles. And, to put the range factor into perspective, even the $25 million Gulfstream G.IV is seldom called upon to fly sectors longer than 1,000 nautical miles.

The present and future picture of the Hawker 1000 is the subject of the final chapter. ✈

Overleaf: Final assembly and ownership of the Hawker family of business jets may be being transferred across the Atlantic, but by no means is the sun setting on the name, as Raytheon presses ahead with production and development of the world-renowned marque.

13

The Raytheon acquisition and the Hawker 800XP

Meanwhile dramatic developments were taking place regarding the ownership of the programme. Back in 1989 British Aerospace's Civil Aircraft Division, of which the Hawker programme was part, split into three separate subsidiary companies, reflecting the three very different markets in which its products were competing. The BAe 146, ATP and Jetstream programmes came under BAe Regional Aircraft, the Airbus programme, for which BAe designs and manufactures the wings, came under BAe Airbus, while BAe Corporate Jets Ltd took on the BAe 125. On 1 May 1992 BAe removed its name from the company and formed Corporate Jets Ltd, and announced that it was seeking a buyer, or at least a majority-ownership partner. In September of that same year, during the NBAA Convention at Dallas, BAe announced that it was withdrawing the company from sale, saying, "We are pleased that the uncertainty surrounding Corporate Jets' future has been removed".

In fact the reason for the announced withdrawal was due to certain difficulties encountered with trying to sell off the company, and these needed to be resolved before any deal could proceed. These included making Corporate Jets a subsidiary of British Aerospace Inc, and moving Corporate Jets' headquarters from Hatfield to the BAe-owned Arkansas Modification Center in Little Rock. US nationals featured strongly in the management team under W.W. (Bill) Boisture, President and CEO, who was appointed in December 1992. Back in the UK the team included: Tom Nicholson, Managing Director Operations; David Laugher, who had been Technical Director since 1989; and Malcolm Bowd, Chief Designer, a post he had taken up on the retirement of Peter Cedervall in 1987.

On 1 June 1993 BAe announced that it had agreed to sell Corporate Jets to Raytheon Company of the USA. Raytheon already owned the Beech Aircraft Corporation, which it had bought in 1980 and which, as detailed in Chapter 6, had once been a partner with Hawker Siddeley on the 125.

The company was given the name Raytheon Corporate Jets Inc, (RCJ). In order to establish a new image for the 125 programme, RCJ,

with the permission of Hawker Siddeley, re-named the aircraft the Hawker 800 and Hawker 1000 (*see Chapter 12*), an acknowledgement to the fact that 125s had been called "Hawkers" by many people for a long time. The first aircraft to officially carry the new name were c/ns 8255 (Hawker 800), and 9043 (Hawker 1000).

In January 1994 RCJ announced that it would fly green Hawker 1000s to Wichita for fitting of avionics and customised interiors. A month later, while actual manufacture of major airframe parts continued at BAe Airbus, assembly was moved across the Chester airfield to a newly refurbished, dedicated facility, which Raytheon leased from BAe.

The most dramatic organisational change occurred in September

The first production Hawker 800XP on an early test flight from Chester in 1995.

The Hawker 800XP, the latest variant of the family and the first launched by Raytheon Aircraft.

1994, when Raytheon Aircraft Company was formed, combining Beech and Hawker into a single $1.7 billion business – this really did complete the circle started in December 1969. Coupled with this news was the announcement of the decision to transfer Hawker production from Chester to Wichita, a process that was to be phased over a period of nearly three years.

The decision had had to be made in response to changing market conditions. Competition in the mid-size cabin market was getting fiercer by the day, with Lear, Citation and Astra all launching new competing models. With cost becoming an ever more vital part of the equation, Raytheon was forced to make the unpalatable decision. As part of BAe, costs and overheads had been shared across a number of civil aircraft programmes, with the Hawker thus benefiting from the resulting economies of scale. As a "stand-alone" company these benefits disappeared and, in spite of a major production cost reduction exercise at Chester, the overall costs of the programme remained too high. The only solution was to move the line, including all engineering and support activities, to Wichita, in order to regain those benefits of scale.

At this same time Tom Nicholson was succeeded by Peter McKee, who now became Managing Director, UK Operations.

While the news of the planned transfer caused understandable concern to those working in the UK, a large number of employees took up the company's offer to relocate to the States – the last thing that Raytheon wanted was to lose all of the valuable skills that were to be found in Hatfield and Chester.

Of some cheer to those who had decided not to move to Kansas was the subsequent decision to develop the Chester Service Centre and retain it at the Broughton site. As Raytheon's first company-owned overseas service facility, it now meets the needs of Hawker operators in Europe, Africa and the Middle East.

Of course, major organisational upheavals could not get in the way of programme development. In early-1995 Raytheon announced an upgraded version of the 800 known as the 800XP (Extended Performance). Harking back to the proposed Series 800I (see Chapter 12), the Hawker 800XP is fitted with TFE 731-5BR engines, giving significant performance improvements, especially for operations from hot and/or short airfields. The new engine has a mixer nozzle and minor materials improvements to raise static thrust to 4,660 lb. The Dee Howard reverser, which previously had been an option but on the 800XP is a standard fit, is relatively unchanged. The basic -5B engine was originally certificated in 1990, so the -5BR came to the 800 as a mature engine. Performance improvements include a speed increase of between five and 14 knots, an improved climb capability (giving a time of just 26 minutes to 37,000 feet at MTOW (ISA + 10), a 19 per cent improvement), and increased design weights. The environmental system is also improved to provide quicker cooling times on the ground and lower ramp noise levels.

Aerodynamically, the 800XP benefits from what is, at first sight, the wing from the Hawker 1000, complete with that aircraft's underwing 'vortilons' in place of the traditional wing fences. However the wing differs structurally, as the 1000 is a heavier aircraft.

As part of the development programme aircraft c/n 8213 was retrofitted with -5BR engines, while aircraft 8266 became the first, pre-series production 800XP. The first true production 800XP was aircraft 8277, which flew for the first time on 5 April 1995. The 800XP made its public debut at the NBAA convention in Las Vegas in September 1995, an occasion which also marked the first customer handover.

On 1 August 1995, the Type Certificate for the Hawker/125 family was transferred from the CAA to FAA jurisdiction, exactly 31 years and 3 days after the original C of A had been issued. The aircraft was now truly American.

In January 1996, the remaining group of Hawker design engineers were moved from Hatfield to Raytheon's European head office building in Harrow. Thus ended the 125's 36-year affiliation with the Hatfield site. Indeed it was the close of an era, marking the end of some 65 years of continuous aircraft design at Hatfield, from the Moths of the early 1930s, through famous, some even may say epoch-making types, such as the Mosquito, Comet and Vampire, to the 125 itself.   ✈

Patriotic pair. BAe promoted the "British" aspect of the Hawker by painting the tails of its US demonstrator aircraft in the colours of the Union Jack. In an unconscious prediction of the future, BAe subsequently changed the colours on these aircraft to the Stars and Stripes.

14
What next?

The immediate future (during 1997) will see the completion of the transition of the Hawker line from Chester to Wichita. The new assembly line in Wichita's Plant IV, located in a $8.5 million, 230,000 sq ft extension, came on stream in late-1995, with aircraft c/n 8297 being the first in the jigs. Throughout 1996 the two lines worked in parallel, most aircraft being produced at Chester ,while Wichita built up experience and speed. Both lines are supplied with fuselage and wing assemblies made by British Aerospace (Airbus), which continues as sub-contractors to the programme. Chester-assembled aircraft are flown out to Wichita "green" for systems installation, with all Hawkers then going to Little Rock for completion and delivery. The plan is that during 1997 production at Chester will progressively run down as the production rate at Wichita accelerates. This is the first time that an aircraft assembly line has been moved from one country to another while a constant production output is maintained.

The Hawker has always made an ideal platform for special mission roles *(see Chapter 11 and Appendix 7)*, the 800 particularly as the C-29A and U-125A variants, as well as the P.134 and P.135 projects, testify. This is a major market for the Hawker and one in which Raytheon Aircraft intends to remain very active. Indeed, as this book closed for press, Raytheon announced that the Republic of Korea has selected the Hawker 800XP for military reconnaissance duties. Eight suitably-equipped aircraft are to be acquired for this role.

Of course, the 800XP is capable of carrying other systems, for example

LOROP (LOng-Range Oblique Photography) cameras or large-format vertical cameras for mapping and surveying, or atmospheric research. In fact the possibilities are endless. The Hawker's amazing versatility, thanks due largely to its structural integrity, coupled with Raytheon/Beech's considerable experience in selling aircraft to governments, would indicate a successful future for special mission Hawkers.

It has been recognised for many years that the 125/Hawker, like any other aircraft design, has a finite development potential. Engineering Director David Laugher says, "We have to question any major change which extends range without holding or increasing cruising speed. To get both requires a new wing." Thus, for five years in the late 1980s, work went ahead at BAe on the "NBJ" (New Business Jet). It was to be

The first US-built Hawker, c/n 8297, on the line in Raytheon Aircraft's newly extended Plant IV in Wichita, in late-1995.

The new Hawker assembly hall at Wichita.

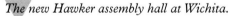

outset has had the strategic vision to wish to realise the full potential of the existing Hawker line.

Until the BAe 1000 was introduced, each new model had always been the replacement for its predecessor. Now Raytheon Aircraft has two models which are developing in parallel. The Hawker 800XP, which superseded the 800 and which was the first variant of Hawker developed by Raytheon Aircraft, is selling well. The Hawker 1000, at a price roughly $3 million higher, offers greater sector distance with increased capacity for passengers and baggage, and a growing proportion of customers want these attributes. However Raytheon, which has invested $372 million in the acquisition of this aircraft family, recognises that the 1000 needs to offer still greater benefits if it is to dominate the "super-mid-size" market, especially since the Hawker 800XP "closed the gap" between the two variants.

As this book goes to print, no decision has yet been announced as to the next generation of 1000, and in a highly competitive market too much cannot be revealed. However Raytheon Aircraft President, Roy

Raytheon Aircraft invested $8.5 million in a 230,000 sq ft extension to its Plant IV facility in Wichita. This photo shows work on the extension during 1995.

an entirely new aircraft, with a 96-inch diameter fuselage and an engine from CFE (the joint AlliedSignal/General Electric company), Pratt & Whitney Canada or Allison. The objective was Gulfstream G.IV performance (4,000-plus nautical miles at Mach 0.8) for the price of a Challenger. This would have been entirely achievable, but British Aerospace now did not consider making business aeroplanes to be "core business", and lacked the appetite to invest £500 million in the future, so the NBJ was shelved. This unquestionably gave impetus to the eventual sale of its Corporate Aircraft Division, and threw into sharp focus the longer-term requirement for investment. Unlike BAe, Raytheon Aircraft does see making business aeroplanes as core business, and from the

Raytheon's Little Rock facility. Today all Hawkers are completed here.

Raytheon's Broughton, Chester, facility. After the assembly line has moved in 1997 this will remain as a company-owned service centre for Hawkers operating in Europe, Africa. and the Middle East.

Norris, has said that: "We are working on an aircraft that would be considerably larger and faster than the current Hawker 1000, and would make extensive use of advanced design, construction and production techniques. Raytheon Aircraft has used customer focus groups to thoroughly define the new airplane. We believe the time spent with these operators has resulted in a truly customer-driven aircraft that will pay off with tremendous success in the market."

With the wonderful benefit of hindsight going back over 35 years, Martin Sharp's "optimistic" press release of 1961 has turned out to be far too pessimistic. Of one thing we can be sure, that with the 800XP newly into service and a 1000 follow-on soon to be announced, the Hawker family will continue to dominate the market – as it has done for the past three decades – for many more years yet to come. And while this book aspires to tell a complete story and to fill a serious gap on aviation bookshelves, it will certainly be many years before the truly definitive history of the 125 can be written ✈ ✈

Appendices

Contents

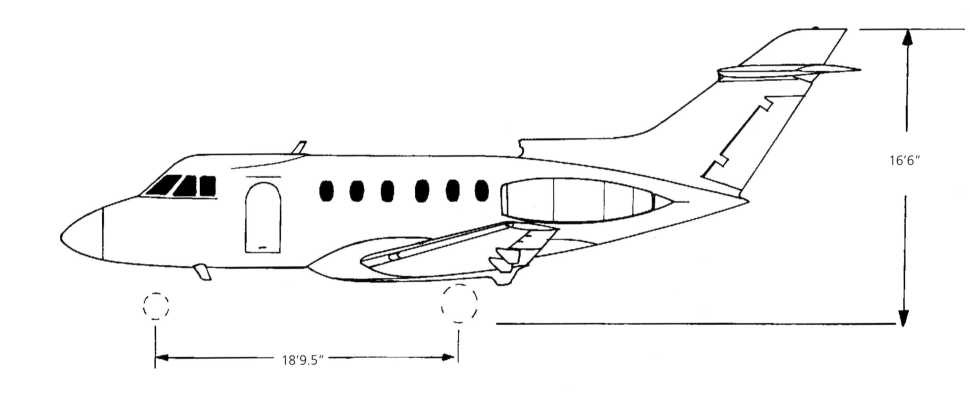

16'6"

18'9.5"

125 Series 1

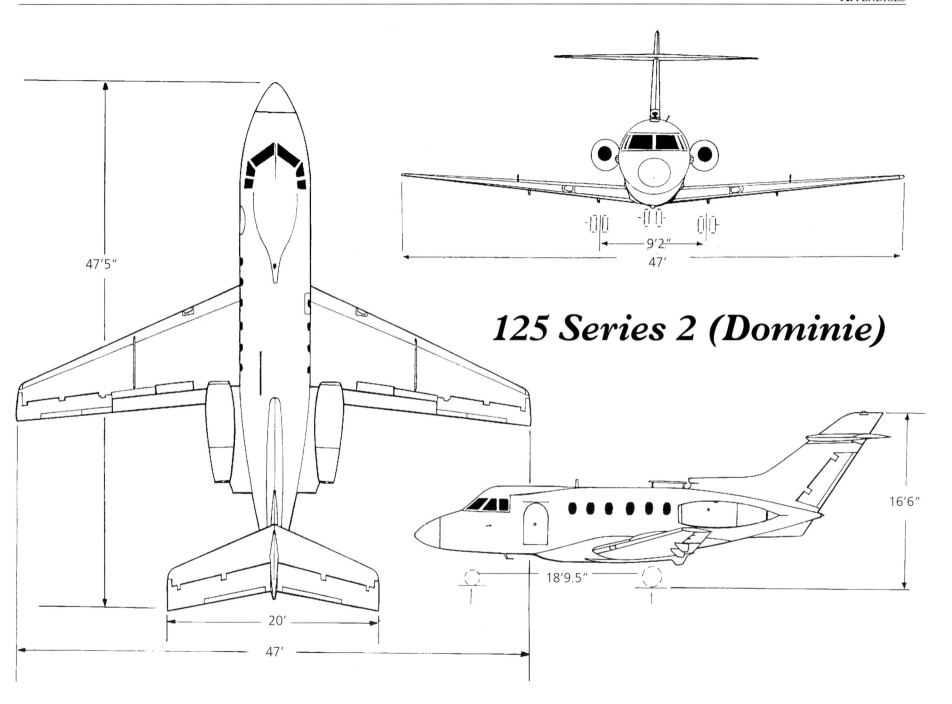

47'5"

9'2"

47'

125 Series 2 (Dominie)

16'6"

18'9.5"

20'

47'

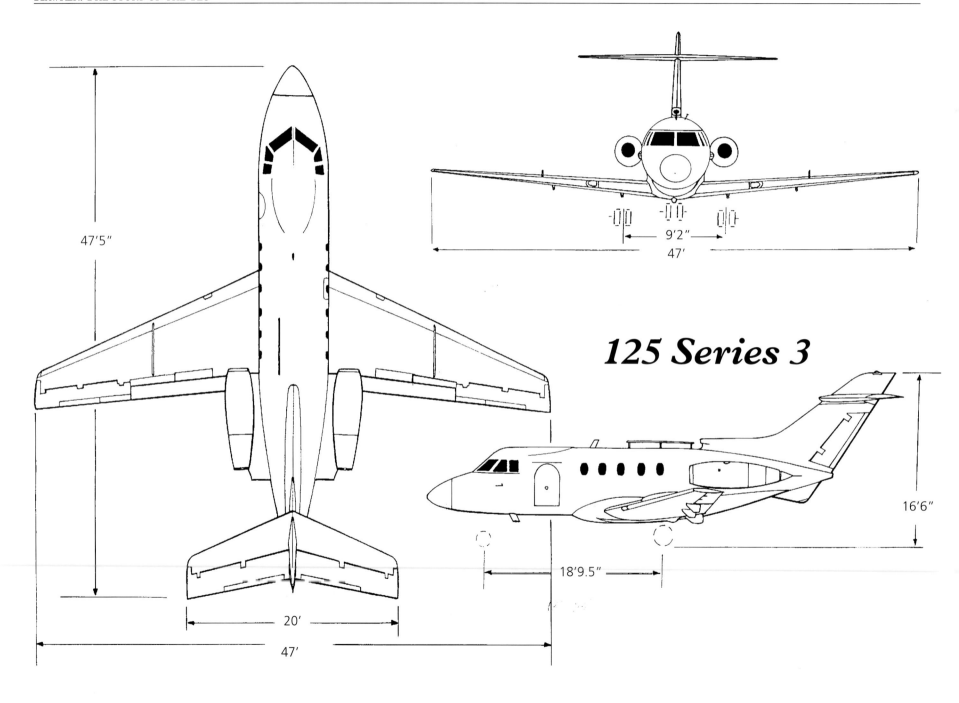

125 Series 3

47'5"

47'

9'2"

47'

20'

47'

18'9.5"

16'6"

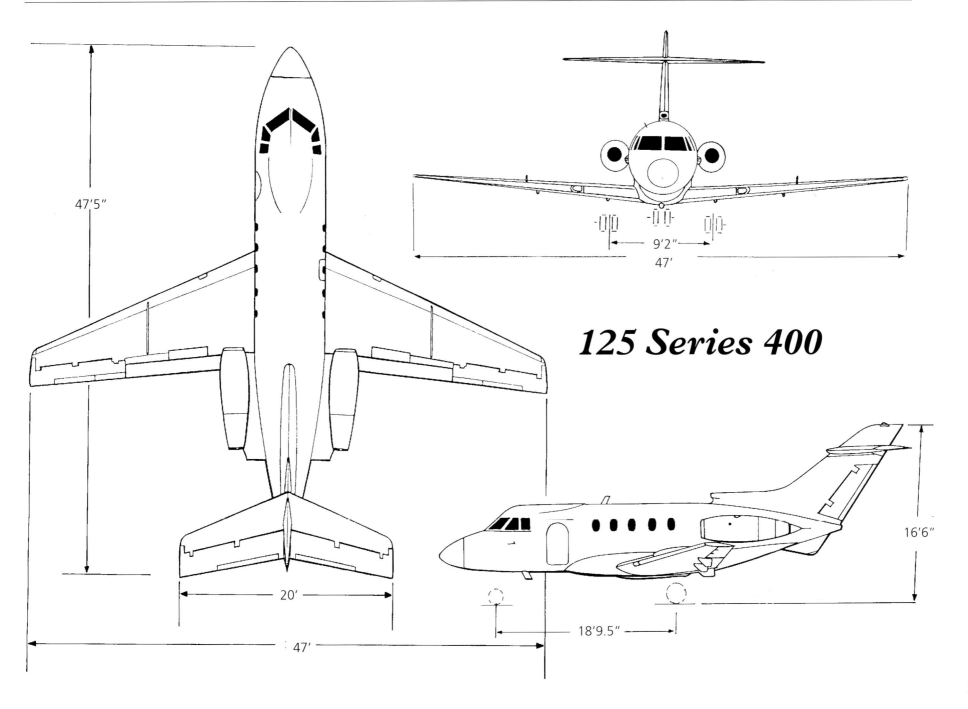

47'5"

9'2"

47'

125 Series 400

16'6"

20'

18'9.5"

47'

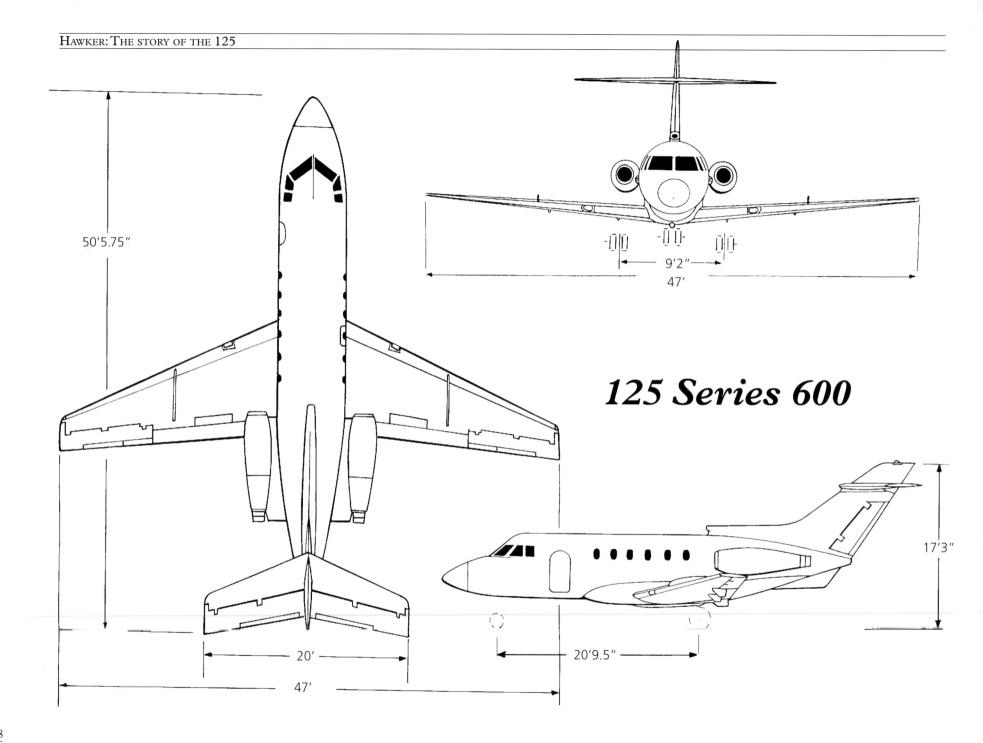

50'5.75"

9'2"

47'

125 Series 600

17'3"

20'

47'

20'9.5"

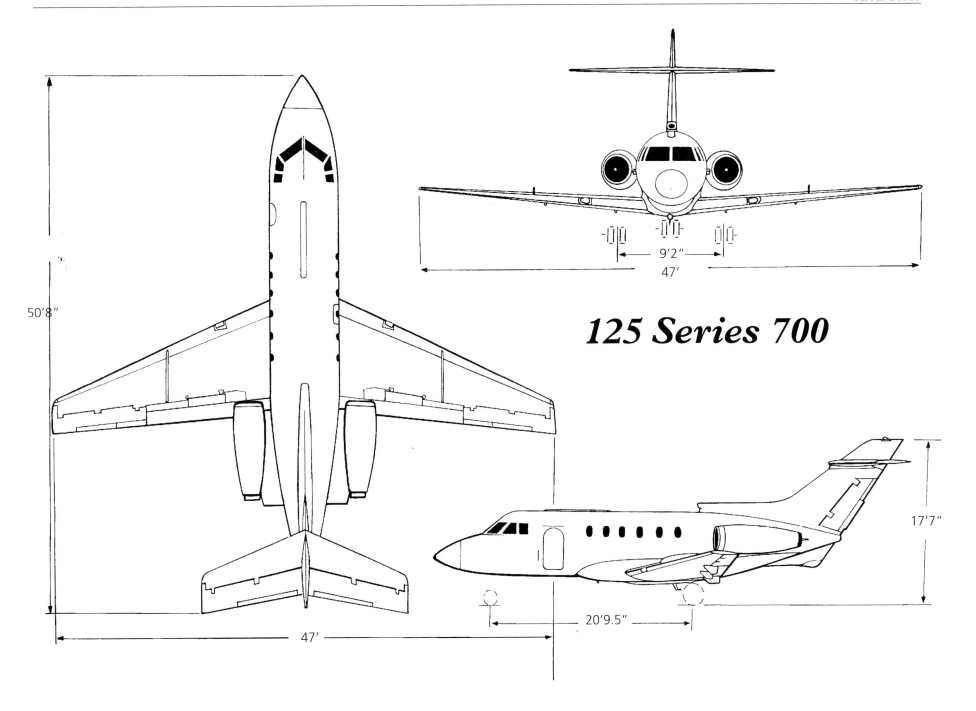

50'8"

9'2"

47'

125 Series 700

17'7"

20'9.5"

47'

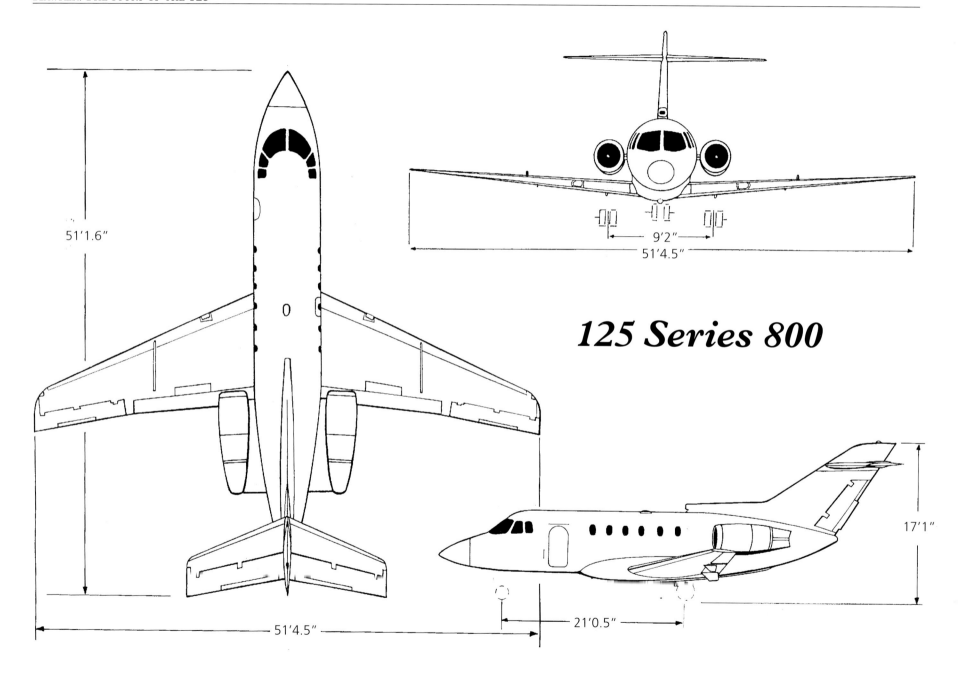

51'1.6"

9'2"

51'4.5"

125 Series 800

17'1"

51'4.5"

21'0.5"

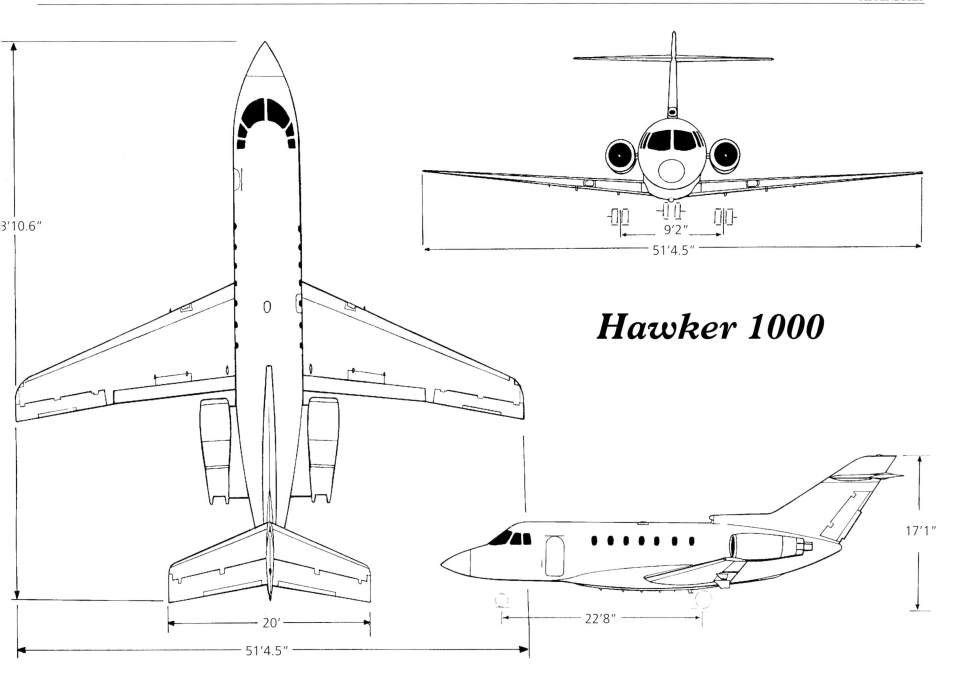

3'10.6"

9'2"

51'4.5"

Hawker 1000

17'1"

20'

22'8"

51'4.5"

Appendix 2

The Hawker heritage

This chart follows the progression of ownership of the Hawker/125 programme since its inception.
Bold type denotes the actual name of the company under which the business was operating at the time:

Up to 1960	**de Havilland Aircraft Co.**
1960	Amalgamation of UK aircraft industry.
	Hawker Siddeley Aviation - de Havilland Division.
1963	**Hawker Siddeley Aviation.**
1977 (29th April)	Nationalisation.
	Aircraft and Shipbuilding Industries Act 1977 established - **British Aerospace.**
1978 (1st January)	Undertakings of individual companies acquired by BAe.
	British Aerospace Aircraft Group, Hatfield/Chester Division.
1981	Denationalisation
	Just over 50% of shares sold by HMG.
1982	**British Aerospace Aircraft Group - Civil Division.**
1984	**British Aerospace Aircraft Group.**
1985	HMG sells remaining shareholding.
	British Aerospace - Civil Aircraft Division.
1989 (1st January)	**British Aerospace (Commercial Aircraft) Ltd - Corporate Aircraft Division.**
1992 (1st January)	**British Aerospace Corporate Jets Ltd.**
1992 (1st May)	**Corporate Jets Ltd.**
	Company offered for sale.
1992 (22nd September)	Company withdrawn from sale.
1992 (1st December)	Company becomes a subsidiary of BAe, Inc.
	Headquarters established in Little Rock, Arkansas. **Corporate Jets, Inc.**
1993 (1st June)	BAe agrees sale of Corporate Jets, Inc. to Raytheon Company.
1993 (6th August)	Raytheon completes acquisition of Corporate Jets, Inc. **Raytheon Corporate Jets, Inc.**
1994 (15th September)	Full amalgamation with Beech Aircraft Company.
	Raytheon Aircraft Company name introduced.
	(UK operation retains Raytheon Corporate Jets name operating as a subsidiary of Raytheon Aircraft Company)

Genealogy

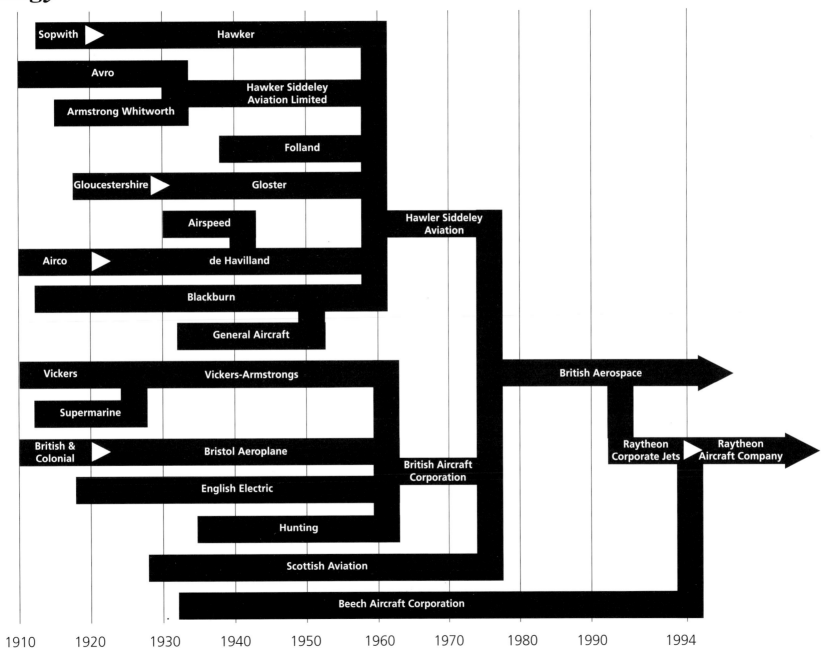

Sopwith ▷ Hawker

Avro

Armstrong Whitworth

Hawker Siddeley
Aviation Limited

Folland

Gloucestershire ▷ Gloster

Airspeed

Airco ▷ de Havilland

Blackburn

General Aircraft

Hawler Siddeley
Aviation

Vickers Vickers-Armstrongs

Supermarine

British & Colonial ▷ Bristol Aeroplane

British Aircraft
Corporation

British Aerospace

Raytheon
Corporate Jets ▷ Raytheon
Aircraft Company

English Electric

Hunting

Scottish Aviation

Beech Aircraft Corporation

1910   1920   1930   1940   1950   1960   1970   1980   1990   1994

Appendix 3

Specification and performance

	Jet Dragon (1960)	Prototypes	Series 1	Series 1A/B	Series 2	Series 3A/B	Series 3ARA/BRA
Overall length	47'	43' 6"	47' 5"	47' 5"	47' 5"	47' 5"	47' 5"
Wingspan	47' 9"	44'	47'	47'	47'	47'	47'
Overall height		14'	16' 6"	16' 6"	16' 6"	16' 6"	16' 6"
Cabin volume (cu.ft.)	630	548	565	565	565	565	565
Engine	RB.145	Viper 511/520	Viper 520	Viper 521 / 522	Viper 301	Viper 522	Viper 522
Thrust (lb)	2,750	2,500/3,000	3,000	3,120 / 3,360	3,000	3,360	3,360
Max ramp weight (lb)			20,100	21,200	21,200	21,700	22,800
MTOW (lb)	17,710	19,000	20,000	21,200	20,500	21,700	22,700/22,800
Operating weight (lb)	8,880		11,100	11,400	11,700	11,500	12,000
Max. payload (lb)			1,800	1,600	1,300	2,000	1,870
Max. payload / full fuel (lb)			800	1,700	1,200	2,000	1,670
Fuel capacity (lb)			7,800	8,200	8,200	8,200	9,100
IFR range (6 Pax – 1,200 lb) (nm)	1,000	900	1,005	1,280	1,110	1,310	1,250
Max. cruise speed (mph)			485	472	472	508	
Balanced field length (SL ISA)	3,700		5,100	4,600 / 4,190	4,700	4,200	4,820
Climb to 35,000 ft (ISA, min)	30		28	28	34	22	24
Service ceiling (ft)			36,000	37,000 / 39,000	39,000	39,000	41,000
First flight	-	13 Aug 62	12 Feb 63	24 Aug 64	30 Dec 64	2 Dec 65	17 Dec 66

Specification and performance

	Series 400A/B / Series 403A/B	Series 600A/B	Series 700A/B	Hawker 800	Hawker 800XP	Hawker 1000
Overall length	47' 5"	50' 6"	50' 8.5"	51' 2"	51' 2"	53' 11"
Wingspan	47'	47'	47'	51' 5"	51' 5"	51' 5"
Overall height	16' 6"	17' 3"	17' 7"	17' 7"	17' 7"	17' 1"
Cabin volume (cu ft)	565	604	604	604	604	680
Engine	Viper 522	Viper 601	TFE731-3R	TFE731-5R	TFE731-5BR	PWC 305B
Thrust (lb)	3,360	3,750	3,700	4,300	4,660	5,225
Max. ramp weight (lb)	23,300	25,000	25,500	27,520	28,120	31,100
MTOW (lb)	23,300 / 23,800	25,000	25,500	27,400	28,000	31,000
Operating weight (lb)	12,295	13,615	14,000	15,120	16,100	18,000
Max. payload (lb)	1,905	1,930	2,300	2,000	2,350	2,300
Max. payload / full fuel (lb)	1,905	1,930	2,060	1,520	2,020	1,660
Fuel capacity (lb)	9,100	9,450	9,440	10,000	10,000	11,440
IFR range (6 pax – 1,200 lbs) (nm)	1,505	1,570	2,300	2,454	2,474	3,044
Max. cruise speed (mph)	508	526	508	509	513	521
Balanced field length (SL, ISA)	4,970	5,000	5,600	5,625	5,510	5,950
Climb to 35,000 ft (ISA, min)	24	21	19	21	18	19
Service ceiling (ft)	41,000	41,000	41,000	41,000*	41,000*	43,000
First flight	23 Aug 68	21 Jan 71	28 Jun 76	26 May 83	1 Sep 94	16 Jun 90

★ CAA cert. to 43,000 ft.

Appendix 4

125/Hawker variants and numbers built

This list details all variants of Hawker/125s that have been built over the years. It includes engine retrofits but not other changes made subsequent to manufacture (e.g. a number of aircraft over the years have been converted from "A" build standard to "B" and vice versa).

Information is accurate as of early-1996.

Model/Series (designation as at time of build)	Engines	Numbers built	Remarks
DH 125 Prototype	Viper 511 / 520	2	
HS 125-1	Viper 520	8	
HS 125-1 (521)	Viper 521	(1 Retrofit)	
DH 125-1A	Viper 521	33	
DH 125-1A/522	Viper 522	28	
DH 125-1A (522)	Viper 522	(10 Retrofits)	
DH 125-1A/S-522	Viper 522	3	
HS 125-1B	Viper 521	3	
HS 125-1B/522	Viper 522	8	
HS 125-1B/R-522	Viper 522	1	Long-range tank
HS 125-1B/S-522	Viper 522	1	
HS 125-1A (Retrofit)	Garrett TFE731-3R-1H	(11 Retrofits)	
HS 125-1A/S (Retrofit)	Garrett TFE731-3R-1H	(2 Retrofits)	
HS 125-2 (Dominie)	Viper 301	20	
HS 125-3	Viper 521	2	Qantas. Later converted to 3B
DH 125-3A	Viper 522	12	

Model/Series (Designation as at Time of Build)	Engines	Numbers Built	Remarks
HS 125-3B	Viper 522	15	
HS 125-3A (Retrofit)	Garrett TFE731-3R-1H	(5 Retrofits)	
HS 125-F3B	Garrett TFE731-3R-1H	(1 Retrofit)	
DH 125-3A/R	Viper 522	2	
DH 125 3A/RA	Viper 522	18	
HS 125-3B/RA	Viper 522	16	
HS 125-3A/RA (Retrofit)	Garrett TFE731-3R-1H	(4 Retrofits)	
HS 125-F3B/RA	Garrett TFE731-3R-1H	(2 Retrofits)	
DH 125-400A	Viper 522	66	Some of these were marketed as BH 125-400s
HS 125-400B	Viper 522	33	
DH 125-403A(C)	Viper 522	4	
HS 125-403B	Viper 522	13	
HS 125-400A (Retrofit)	Garrett TFE731-3R-1H	(51 Retrofits)	
HS 125-F400B	Garrett TFE731-3R-1H	(8 Retrofits)	
HS 125-600A	Viper 601	33	24 of these were sold as BH 125-600s
HS 125-600B	Viper 601	40	Includes 1 development aircraft never sold
HS 125-600A (Retrofit)	Garrett TFE731-3R-1H	(7 Retrofits)	
HS 125-F600B	Garrett TFE731-3R-1H	(6 Retrofits)	
HS 125-700A / BAe 125-700A	Garrett TFE731-3R-1H	143	Includes 1 aircraft upgraded and marketed as a BAe 125-700-II
HS 125-700B / BAe 125-700B	Garrett TFE731-3R-1H	72	
BAe 125-800A / BAe 125-800B / Corporate 800 / Hawker 800	Garrett TFE731-5R-1H	273	Includes one aircraft (8213) subsequently converted to 800XP standard
Hawker 800XP	Garrett TFE731-5BR-1H	(7)	Production continuing
BAe 1000★ / Corporate 1000★ / Hawker 1000	PW305B	(45)	Production continuing

★ Marketing designation only. Type certificate shows BAe 125 Series 1000.

Appendix 5

Deliveries by year

	125/ Hawker	Falcon 20/200	Sabre-liner	Lear 55 / 60	Citation III /VI /VII	Astra
1963	2		4			
1964	8		23			
1965	44	15	28			
1966	57	51	36			
1967	21	57	29			
1968	33	43	25			
1969	32	26	33			
1970	39	25	12			
1971	27	19	9			
1972	21	30	16			
1973	30	24	26			
1974	17	21	42			
1975	10	23	28			
1976	14	16	28			
1977	23	18	26			
1978	32	22	24			
1979	31	21	15			
1980	35	16	41			

	125/ Hawker	Falcon 20/200	Sabre- liner	Lear 55 / 60	Citation III /VI /VII	Astra
1981	37	24	37	15		
1982	29	7	2	53		
1983	18	12	1	24	18	
1984	27	11		16	50	
1985	27	10		7	28	1
1986	27	5		7	21	7
1987	31	6		4	26	1
1988	30	1		2	15	8
1989	32	2		6	16	11
1990	29	2		4	15	9
1991	16			2	16	11
1992	30				26	6
1993	29			16	24	8
1994	21			22	24	6
1995	34			24	15	?

New Hawkers have been sold into 45 countries worldwide and an additional 16 countries have bought used aircraft.

Source of data: British Aerospace/GAMA

Appendix 6

Military designations

Designation	*Air arm*	*Role*	*Series*
Dominie T.1	Royal Air Force	Navigation training	2
Mercurius	South African Air Force	VIP/Communications	400B
CC.1 / 1A	Royal Air Force	VIP/Communications	400B /F400B
CC.2 / 2A	Royal Air Force	VIP/Communications	600B /F600B
CC.3	Royal Air Force	VIP/Communications	700B
C-29A	United States Air Force / F.A.A.	Flight inspection	800A
CF-X) U-125)	Japan Air Self Defence Force	Flight inspection	800B
HS-X) U-125A)	Japan Air Self Defense Force	Search & rescue	800

Appendix 7

Special variants

While the Hawker is potentially capable of fulfilling a wide range of duties, to date the following roles have been met by aircraft specifically adapted or modified for the task:

Navigator training

Pilot training

VIP transport and government communications

Air ambulance (both dedicated and convertible)

Flight inspection (both dedicated and convertible)

Systems development (avionics, noise, mission equipment...)

Noise measurement

Atmospheric-gas measurement

Maritime search and rescue